The
FOCALGUIDE
to
Photographing
Places

THE ⓕ FOCALGUIDES TO

Basic Photography
COLOUR   David Lynch
EFFECTS AND TRICKS   Günter Spitzing
EXPOSURE   David Lynch
LIGHTING   Paul Petzold
LOW LIGHT PHOTOGRAPHY   Paul Petzold
SELLING YOUR PHOTOGRAPHS   Ed Buziak
SLIDES   Graham Saxby

Equipment
CAMERA ACCESSORIES   Leonard Gaunt
CAMERAS   Clyde Reynolds
FILTERS   Clyde Reynolds
FLASH   Günter Spitzing
LARGER FORMAT CAMERAS   Sidney Ray
LENSES   Leonard Gaunt
SLIDE-TAPE   Brian Duncalf
35 mm   Leonard Gaunt
THE 35mm SINGLE-LENS REFLEX   Leonard Gaunt

Processing
CIBACHROME   Jack H. Coote
COLOUR FILM PROCESSING   Derek Watkins
COLOUR PRINTING   Jack H. Coote
THE DARKROOM   Leonard Gaunt
ENLARGING   Günter Spitzing
HOME PROCESSING   Ralph Jacobson

Subjects
ACTION PHOTOGRAPHY   Don Morley
BIRD PHOTOGRAPHY   Michael W. Richards
CLOSE-UPS   Sidney Ray
MOUNTAINS   Douglas Milner
PHOTOGRAPHING PEOPLE   Alison Trapmore
PHOTOGRAPHING PLACES   D. H. Day
PLANTS AND FLOWERS   David Walton
PORTRAITS   Günter Spitzing
WEDDINGS & SPECIAL OCCASIONS   Bob Bluffield

Movie
MOVIEMAKING   Paul Petzold
SHOOTING ANIMATION   Zoran Perisic

The FOCALGUIDE to Photographing Places

D. H. Day

Focal Press · London

Focal/Hastings House · New York

British Library Cataloguing in Publication Data

Day, D H
   Focalguide to photographing places.
   1. Photography – Landscapes
   I. Title
   778.9′4   TR660

ISBN (excl. USA) 0 240 50960 9
ISBN (USA only) 0 8038 2353 3

Text set in 10/12 pt Photon Univers printed and bound
in Great Britain at The Pitman Press, Bath

Contents

Preparing Your Equipment   9
What to take   9
Checking the gear   10
Simple cameras   10
Complex cameras   11

Planning Pictures and Finding Them   13
Composing a picture   15
If in doubt, leave it out!   16
Composition   18
Looking through the viewfinder   20
Selecting the lens to use   22
Wide-angle lens   23
Telephoto lens   24
Finding pictures   24
Finding subjects   26
Looking at other people's pictures   28
Picture formats   29

Exposure   31
What is exposure?   31
Shutter speeds   31
Lens apertures   32
Combinations   32
Measuring exposure   34
Separate meters   36
Incident light metering   38
Built-in meters   40
Automatic exposure control   42
Auto-exposure with selection   44
Exposure override controls   45

General hints 46
Difficult subjects 46
If you are desperate 47
Pre-exposure checklist 48

Landscapes 49
What is in a view? 49
Depth and perspective 50
Setting up the shot 52
Taking the shot 52
A second shot 55
Bubbling waters 56
Slowing down 58
Still waters 59
Fisheyes and the like 61
Panoramas 61
Light, sun and seasons 64
Sunrises and sunsets 66
Exposure 67
Building your own pictures 69

Buildings 71
Leaving buildings in their proper light 71
What is it made of? 72
Cross-lighting on brickwork 73
Which way does the building face? 73
Clouds 73
What else is around? 74
Constructive shadows 74
Do not look up! 76
Do look up! 78
Using the foreground 78
Selecting a lens 80
More ways than one 81
Buildings in a landscape 82
Looking through 82
Buildings after dark 86
Churches and cathedrals 86

Indoors   88
Houses and smaller buildings   89
People and buildings   90

Townscapes   91
Buildings   91
Famous landmarks   94
Streets and squares   94
Activity on the streets   95
Industry   96
Traffic and transport   97
People in townscapes   100
Keeping out of trouble   101
The sum of the parts   101

Coasts and Beaches, Mountains and Snow 102
Coasts and beaches   102
Simple snapshots   103
Full-scale photography   103
Exposures   104
Beyond the beach ball   106
People again!   107
Harbours   107
All at sea   108
Shooting against the light   111
Snow and ice   112
Sun and skylight   114
Photography in the cold   114
Mountains   116
Climbing mountains   118

Pictures after Dark   120
Films at night   120
Long exposures   122
Street lighting   122
Picturing light   123
Floodlit buildings   124
Moving lights   125

Lightning   125
Moonlight   126
Indoors at night   127
What about the colour?   127
Sports   128
Entertainments   130
Flash   130
Painting with light   131

What Sort of Equipment?   132
Simple cameras   132
35mm cameras   133
Cameras   133
Single-lens reflex (SLR) or rangefinder? 134

Lenses   134
Maximum lens apertures   138
Roll-film (120) cameras   139
Gadgets   141
Polarizing filters   142
Contrast filters   142
Haze filters   146
Gadget bags   146
Tripods   147

Choosing a Film   149
Choosing a colour film   150
Film speeds   152
Colour balance   152
Slide films   154
Choosing a black-and-white film   156
Looking after your films   157
Keep in a cool dry place   157
Taking your film through airports   158

Index   159

Preparing your Equipment

Learning to be a photographer involves two separate processes: the first is learning about the equipment and how to get the best out of it. The second part is learning how to take pictures. That means looking through the viewfinder and getting the picture you really want. Of course, no one succeeds every time; I have never met a photographer who could do that; but a good photographer can get acceptable pictures most of the time and very good pictures regularly. You can learn how to operate a camera anywhere, but you can learn to take real pictures only by going to look for them. Learn from the pictures you have taken yourself, and read magazines and books. If you can go out with a more experienced photographer and watch him work, then go, because it is undoubtedly the best way of learning, once you have mastered the basic skills.

In fact that is the way most professionals learn their craft. They start as a photographer's assistant, and spend two years loading and unloading cameras, carrying bags of camera gear, taking exposure meter readings and many other 'chores'. They do everything except take pictures. It is a fairly frustrating life, and it is only when they start as photographers in their own right that they discover just how many tricks, and how many techniques they have learned, just by watching and making sure that they have the right equipment for the assignment, and the right sort and amount of film. If you do not run to an assistant you have to check your own gear, and you have to do it every time. It does not matter how simple or complicated your camera equipment is, make sure it is clean and working before you set out. It can save a wasted trip, or a lot of frustration.

What to take

There are many books on the relative advantages and disadvantages of different types, sizes or brands of camera and their accessories.

Here we should just note that you should aim to have with you everything you may need on that trip: but not to lug bags full of unused equipment around the world. Just as each picture should be your personal decision on the best way to show your subject, so each outfit should be your decision on the best way to be in a position to secure the pictures you want.

For example, if someone offers to take you sailing for your first time, take along a simple cheap camera. You can take quick snaps when you have a moment, and a capsize will not be a disaster. On the other hand, if you are going on a world cruise, take every useful piece of equipment that you own, or can borrow or hire. You might need a 7.5mm fisheye lens just once, but if you took one, you have it.

The fortunate few can build up a stock of different camera outfits to suit their different photographic pursuits. The rest of us, however, have to make do with just one outfit. If that is your case, make sure that each item is there for a good purpose.

Checking the gear

Having presumably made a choice of equipment, always check that it is clean and working before you go out. It is the only way of remembering the lens you took out of the gadget bag to clean and left in the bedroom drawer. Before you go on a long trip, have your equipment looked over by an expert repair service. It costs money, but it also saves pictures.

For everyday outings, use the following checklist.

Simple cameras

1 Check there is no film in camera.
2 Open the camera back and dust out with soft brush.
3 Hold this lens towards light and fire shutter. A quick flash of light indicates that the shutter is working. Sometimes there is a small lever inside the back of a 126 camera which has to be pressed before the shutter will work.

4 Check that the lens is clean. If it is not, clean it carefully. Most simple camera lenses are plastic and scratch easily. Brush the dust away from the lens until *all* of it is removed – if you leave any you will scratch the lens. Then gently breathe on the lens and polish it with a 'Selvyt' cloth. These are sold by most photographic dealers and are the only cloth you should ever use on a lens. The corner of a handkerchief might be all right for a professional who frequently changes his lenses, but if you do not want to do the same, never use a handkerchief.

5 Select and load your film.

Complex cameras

1 Check there is no film in camera. With a 35mm camera turn the rewind knob as though you were rewinding a film, but without pressing the rewind button. If you start to feel pressure on the rewind knob, then there is film in the camera.

2 Assuming there is no film, open the camera back and dust out with a soft brush.

3 Turn the wind-on lever to make the shutter work, look through the back, point the camera towards a window and press the shutter. A quick flash of light will show that the shutter is working. This does not test the accuracy of the shutter, but it does show that it is not jammed.

4 Select and load your film. Keep the end flap of the film box to remind you which film is in the camera.

5 35mm only – check that the film is winding on – some cameras have an indicator, with others you can check by looking at the rewind knob.

6 Check the lens. It should be protected by a clean UV filter. If necessary clean it, first with a lens brush and then with lens cleaning fluid to remove any greasy marks, such as fingerprints. If you have to clean the lens itself, be very careful not to scratch it, and *never* use a silicone coated cleaning cloth. The silicone can affect the coated surface of the lens.

7 If you have other lenses, make sure that they too are clean and protected by their own UV filter.

8 Check that all the lens hoods are in their place in the camera case.

9 If your camera has a built-in meter, check the battery, if you have one. If it is exhausted, replace it.

10 If you are going to take a tripod with you, check that the cable-release is in place.

Planning Pictures and Finding Them

The earliest stages of photography are in many ways the most satisfying. Learning to manipulate the controls is easy and comes quickly, and you can measure the results in terms of sharp and correctly exposed pictures with the depth of field you want. Once you have mastered that you can start on the second phase of your photographic career – applying these basic skills in a wide range of situations to give the pictures you want. Concentrating on what you see through the viewfinder and turning that into the most effective picture becomes totally absorbing. Once you can take the mastery of the controls for granted, the ability to look through a viewfinder becomes critical.

Scan almost any magazine on virtually any topic and you will see a bewildering range of pictures – some good and some not so good. Look more carefully and you will see that all the good ones have one thing in common, there is no doubt what the subject of the picture is intended to be. Focus, exposure and composition all lead your eye to the same point, they all make the subject of the picture stand out.

Every photographer must apply those same standards to his work, not only to the finished results but to the subject before he takes it. Always work out quite clearly what the subject of the picture is to be and why you are taking the picture. 'I am going to take a picture of this street to show the different styles and ages of the buildings and that people have been living, working and shopping in them from time immemorial.' Or 'I want to show that this shopping precinct has been designed and built especially for people who are shopping in the 20th Century and that it serves the people who drive rather than walk to the shops'.

By doing that you have a better idea of what to include in the picture and what to leave out. Both pictures need people in them because you want to show that the buildings are still in use. In the first case you probably have to include as many different buildings as possible in the shot because you want to show the conglomeration of buildings of different ages. In the second case you may need to show only one shop, but you still need people in the picture and you should include at least part of the car park. Defining the purpose of the picture has told you that, and it is a feature you might otherwise want to hide. If you can stand back a little and show how the precinct is isolated from the places people live – perhaps in the middle of a desert or an industrial estate – then that too reinforces the automobile-dependent nature of the place.

How often have you been shown photographs taken by people away on a trip somewhere. The commentary is always similar, something about – 'the car park is just out of the picture to the left', or 'you can't quite see it from this picture but if you go a short way up the street ...'. The photographs are usually muddled collections of buildings, people, parked cars, possibly a distant glimpse of an ancient cathedral, and best of all, a blurred figure, which you are told is Aunt Henrietta, disappearing in the middle distance. When the photographer shows you his pictures he has a clear idea of what he wants to bring to your attention, but it often does not appear in the picture. If he had devoted just a little of his time to think about his future commentary *before* he took the picture then the picture would relate it's own story.

There is no way of taking a prize-winning picture of the west front of Rheims Cathedral which also shows the hotel you stayed at and is a perfect outdoor portrait of your wife. Good pictures have only one subject and are taken for only one purpose, probably that purpose is just to make a good picture. But whatever the purpose everything done is aimed at making the subject and the purpose of the picture more unambiguous, clearer and easy to understand. If the commentary with a picture is 'I was trying to show ...' that picture is a failure, take pictures which *do* show what you wanted them to and forget the commentary. Good pictures communicate quickly and easily.

That does not, though, restrict you to taking boring record shots. If you can achieve your purpose better with a silhouette, a misty blur or an abstract array of lights, all well and good. The important thing is to decide just what you want the picture to look like; and to frame that picture in the viewfinder with the camera controls set to give you the right effect on your film.

Before you take a picture, work out clearly what the subject is and you will find that the selection of lens, shutter speed, depth of field, viewpoint and the actual framing within the viewfinder are almost decided for you.

Composing a picture

Consider a particular picture – a view of open rolling countryside. The picture must have one point of interest. If there is nothing for the viewer to rest his eyes on, then he looks frantically round the picture looking for a point of interest, fails to find it and gives up. Always include some point of focus, it might be a church steeple or a farm or a solitary tree, but it gives a focal point to the picture.

Because the picture is of rolling countryside it should have a sense of distance of the countryside rolling away to a distant horizon. To get that feeling of distance in a two-dimensional picture you need to include a nearby object. The difference in size between an overhanging branch, or a gate, and the distant trees and hills allows the viewer to subconsciously make a comparison and he comes up with the right answer – great distances.

As you can see the decision to take a picture of rolling landscape has virtually told you the sort of picture you are looking for. That does not mean that all pictures of landscape are boringly similar, it just means that you have a clear idea of the elements needed for the picture.

The sort of countryside you are in will suggest which lens to use. That may not be very obvious at first, but the pattern becomes clear quite quickly. A compact countryside with a winding river and a narrow valley may suggest a wide-angle lens to include both sides of the valley. With a wide view, perhaps even the widest of lenses will not do justice to the panorama. You can use a short telephoto lens, and select some of the typical features of the view in the narrower angle of view, which will hint at the scenery surrounding the picture without actually showing it. If the features you want to include in your picture are well scattered, say the cottage you want to include as the focal point of the picture is a long way away, then you may want to use a telephoto lens to 'pull' the cottage into the picture.

When you start looking through the viewfinder, the basic elements of the picture are already decided. The foreground usually needs to be sharp and in focus as well as the horizon. The horizon should run, not across the middle of the picture, but towards the top or bottom of the picture; about one-third from the top or the bottom of the picture is the usual rule of composition. You should not hesitate to break rules, because they are designed for perfect landscapes, and many landscapes photograph best if you do break the rules.

If in doubt, leave it out!

Look in the viewfinder for things which do not need to be there. If you come in closer to the foreground, does the picture lose anything, or does it make the picture simpler?

The fewer objects there are in a picture, the more simply it tells its story. Work at removing unneccessary objects from your pictures. Look through the viewfinder, and check off everything you can see in it. What is the purpose of the picture? Does that purpose need that object in it? Does a view need three trees in the foreground, or can you move closer, and shoot between two of the trees. That way you lose the tops of all the trees and all the sky above them. Instead you have interlacing branches, and the view appears between them; the trees form a dark frame for the view of the countryside in front of you. That dark area helps in another way. The darkness makes the light view behind stand out more, increasing the feeling of depth in the picture, and because there is no light around the edge to distract his attention making the viewer move further into the picture. Over to the left in our imaginary location, there is a piece of rusty farm machinery. Does it add anything to the picture? Not in this case, so take a step to the left and hide it behind a hedge. In this way, the number of objects to distract the viewer are reduced, and the picture gains in impact.

Consider all the items in each picture and at first consciously look at each item and decide if it is useful in the picture. Very soon your eye

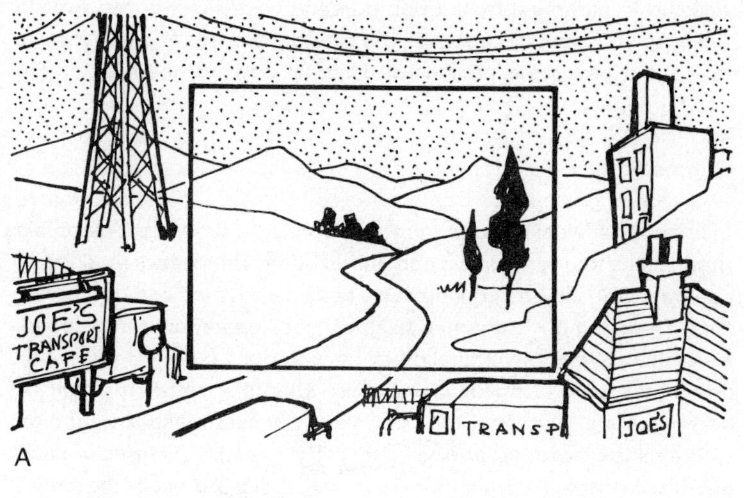

A

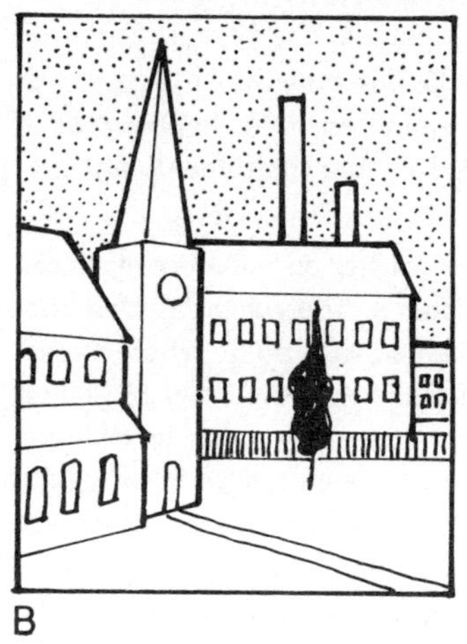

B

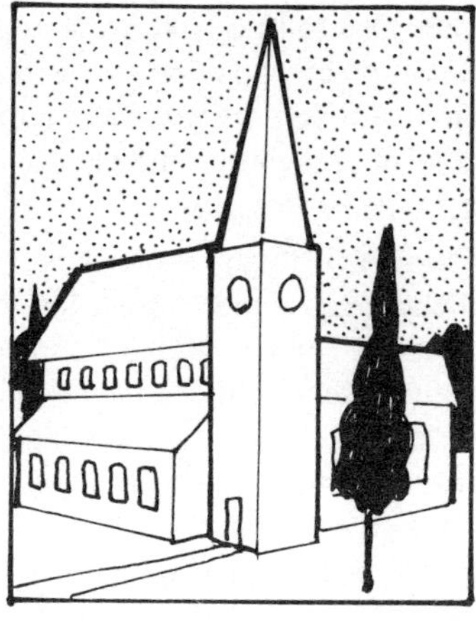

Viewpoint is becoming increasingly important as our world gets more cluttered. A. Sometimes you can select a closer view—perhaps by changing your lens—to avoid problems. B. Walking around your subject can improve the picture beyond recognition.

will become trained into looking at these things and making the decisions without thinking about it. From that point your apprenticeship in photography is at an end and your pictures can expand because you have control over the pictorial content and can start to make your pictures express your personal view of the world.

Composition

Leonardo da Vinci drew a man and from that drawing took all his proportions for works of art and architecture. The Greeks made their columns with slightly curving sides because they look straighter like that. Throughout history man has been looking for, but never found, a simple rule which would allow anyone to draw a perfect picture or design the perfect building. No man without a sense of scale of balance, scale, harmony, tone or colour will ever make a picture as well as a man with great artistic flair. The greatest pictures of each age break the rules which are in vogue. Rules are useful however, they allow most people to make satisfying pictures most of the time. They also form a starting point for the genius.

Rules of composition are a great help but they are made to be broken. If you want to take a picture which does not fit the rules it does not mean that the picture is bad, only that the rules do not suit it.

The rule of thirds is the most common of the compositional dicta. Divide each edge of the picture into thirds. The rules say that the principal point of interest should be placed at a point where these thirds intercept. It is a useful guide particularly in the early stages of composing a picture in the viewfinder, but it can also be restrictive. This is particularly true if you are using a wide-angle lens which places a great deal of emphasis on the foreground. Closely related to this is the 'golden section' so favoured in earlier centuries. The golden section divides each edge not into one-third and two-thirds but in the ratio 618:382. Then the ratio of the longer section to the whole edge is exactly the same. Pictures taken applying the golden section have a still, old-master look to them which is good for some pictures and bad for others.

Composition concerns what happens to a viewer's eye when looking

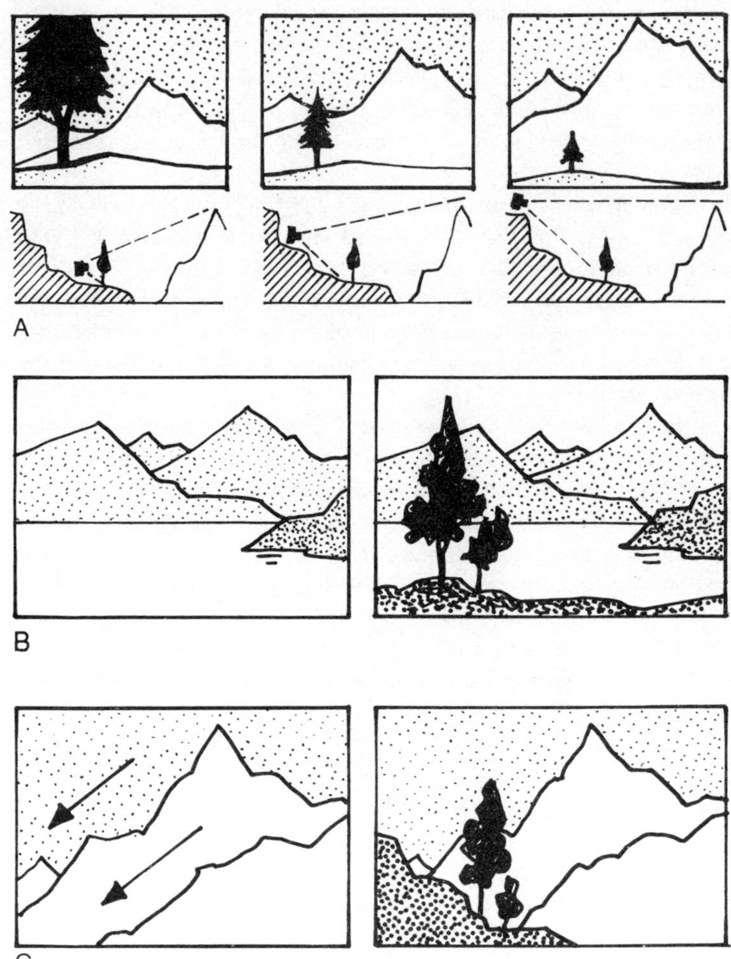

Look carefully at landscapes to be sure of the right view. A. As you move up and away from the foreground, so you increase the domination of the hills behind. B. Try to include enough foreground interest to balance a distant scene. 3 strong diagonals can be irritating unless you include a 'stop'.

at a picture. People do not take the whole of a picture in at once. Their eyes start looking at one point – the point of entry – and move around looking at the various elements of the picture which attract their interest. Eventually they end up at one point – the point of interest – or they slide aimlessly away from the picture and start looking elsewhere. So to make a picture interesting and absorbing, create a point of entry then give a series of clues which direct the eye in the way you want it to move until it arrives at your selected point of interest.

The golden section, by placing the centre of interest obviously nearer to one edge than the other, allows the eye to rest and concentrate on the subject of the picture. If the centre of interest is placed nearer the middle, the viewer's eye starts to judge which edge it is nearer. Distances are compared, and the viewer becomes interested in judging the relative distances instead of looking at the picture itself.

Another rule which is generally useful is that the subject should lead into the picture. A road, hedgerow, wall or river can lead the eye from the edge of the picture towards the centre of interest, this provides a convenient point of entry. This rule can be extended to define what happens near the centre of the picture, and you can have it leading to a single point of interest, or two or three points of interest between which the eye can move in a smooth circular movement. Do the opposite, and have the trees, or river leading out of the picture, and the eye follows the line and is directed smoothly *out* of the picture.

Looking through a viewfinder?

Now it is time to apply the rules when you take your pictures.

First of all, check that there are no visual 'stops' which prevent the eye moving smoothly about the picture. A tree-trunk stretching from top to bottom of the picture, or a power line which stretches across the picture. These are the sort of things which can stop the eye moving in the way it should in a good picture. One of the worst of the visual stops is the horizon. If it is positioned across the middle of the picture, the picture is cut in two. The eye is not sure whether the

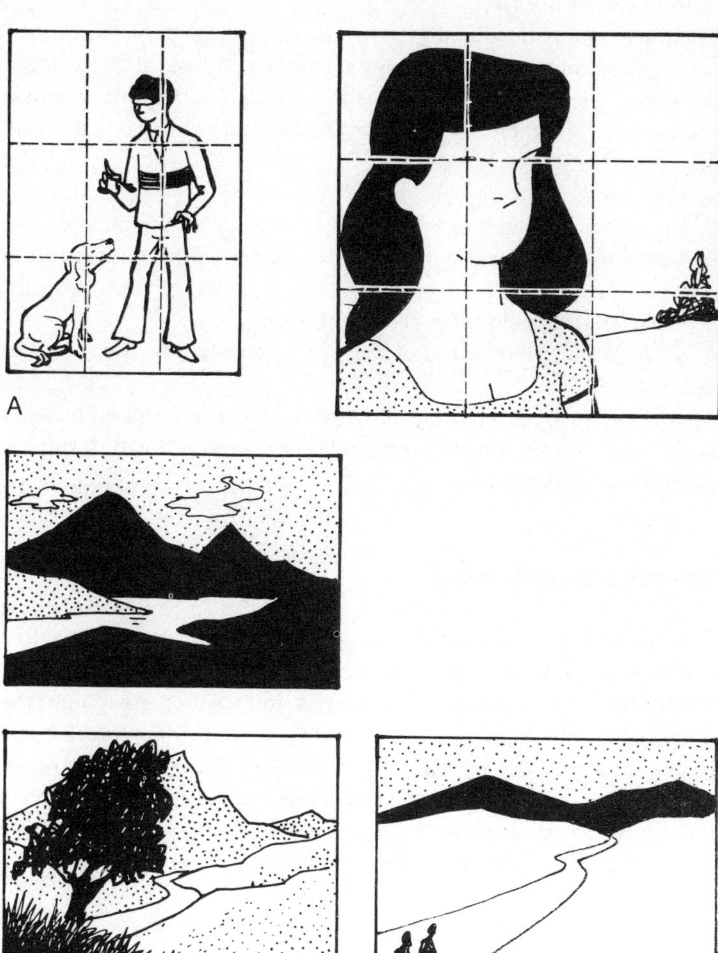

Rules can be a good starting-point for attractive pictures; but many of the best shots ignore them. A. The rule of thirds suggests that you put your subject one third of the way across the frame, and points of interest at the intersections of 'third' lines. B. Diagonals running into the picture give you a settled, tranquil effect.

picture is below that horizon line, or above. So it dodges back and forth between the two.

Compose your picture so that, when you look around the viewfinder, nothing gets in the way of the eye seeing the picture, nothing blocks the view, there are no unexplained shadows which wander across the picture, and there is something of interest for the eye to focus on.

To sum up

1 Never position the horizon across the middle of the picture.

2 Never position the main centre of interest at the middle of the picture.

3 Provide some point of entry into the picture.

4 Arrange the picture so that the eye is led towards the centre of interest.

Bear these rules in mind but remember, many more good pictures have been taken which break rules than have been taken by slavishly applying them.

Selecting the lens to use

If your camera will accept interchangeable lenses, then you have to select a lens for each picture. Sometimes the picture will dictate which lens should be used. Sometimes you have to stand up close and still picture all of your subject; then you have no choice but a wide-angle lens. Conversely, it may not be physically possible to get closer to the subject, so to fill the frame with your chosen subject you must shoot through a long-focus (telephoto) lens. In those cases the only problem is whether you have the right lens with you.

However, there is also a wide range of subjects where you must make a choice of lenses. The selection is normally based on the effect you want in the picture. By 'effect' I mean apparent perspective; perspective is conveyed by the difference in size of objects near to the camera, and objects further away, as they appear in the finished photograph. People generally talk of wide-angle lenses giving 'deep perspective' – objects get smaller very quickly as the distance between them and the subject increases; normal lenses give 'normal perspective' and telephoto lenses give 'compressed perspective' – objects further away from the camera do not become as small as you would expect.

In fact this is not strictly true. What a telephoto lens does is to magnify a small part of the scene until it fills the frame on your camera and a wide-angle lens makes a larger part of the scene smaller, fitting more of the subject into the same frame size. However, if you take a picture on a normal lens and magnify a part of it, then you will see the compressed perspective of a telephoto lens. In fact, at one stage I did not have a telephoto lens and had to do just that whenever my subject was too far away.

In the same way, if you took a series of pictures using a normal lens, and assembled them to cover the same angle of view as a wide-angle lens, you would probably include more foreground objects, and so get deep perspective. So what really controls perspective? Viewpoint controls perspective. If you get very close to a subject you will get the deep perspective associated with wide-angle lenses. When you are using a wide-angle lens you can get closer to the subject and still get all of it in the viewfinder, so you stand closer to the foreground when taking your picture, and get deep perspective. In the same way, stand a long way back from the subject and you get the compressed perspective associated with the telephoto lens.

Wide-angle lens

Obviously, if you cannot stand further back and cannot get the whole subject in the frame using a normal lens, use a wide-angle lens. This also makes the foreground, which appears very large in the picture, the most important element, and separates it clearly from the background, which appears very small.

When composing any picture using a wide-angle lens, pay special attention to the foreground. You must have something to give interest to this area, otherwise the gaping area of foreground will distract the viewer's attention from the remainder of the picture. If this area can be arranged to lead the eye into the picture, so much the better. If you are using a very wide-angle lens, such as a 20mm lens on a 35mm camera, beware of getting your feet in the picture, it is much easier to do than you would believe. Also watch out for your own shadow, or the shadows of someone standing behind you appearing in the bottom part of the picture, they will form a line which leads interest out of the picture, and leaves the viewer more interested in who the shadow belonged to than the intended subject of the picture.

Telephoto lens

Use a telephoto lens if you cannot get closer to the subject, and want to fill the frame. Use a telephoto lens also when you wish distant objects to appear closer, and form a more important part of the composition. The pictures have a 'huddled' close-together feel, and the telephoto lens is almost irresistable when photographing city streets, when trying to convey the closed-in feeling any city gives. Again quoting for a 35mm camera, I would suggest that a 135mm lens gives almost equal emphasis to the foreground and background. Use a longer focal length lens, and the background begins to be more dominant than the foreground.
Do not forget, if you do not have a telephoto lens, use a normal lens, stand further back from the subject, then mask down the processed picture. This is easy if you make your own prints, but not quite so easy with transparencies.

Finding pictures

The keen amateur does not *have* to take pictures and he can choose his own subjects; so how do you set about finding subjects for your pictures?
Really only three sorts of photograph are ever taken: snaps, perfect pictures, and pictures with a purpose.
Snaps are a record of what your family and friends did, and where they went. They are one of the most enjoyable sorts of picture to look back on; but do not waste time taking them on an expensive fully adjustable camera, buy a cartridge-loading camera and stop worrying about exposure and depth of field.

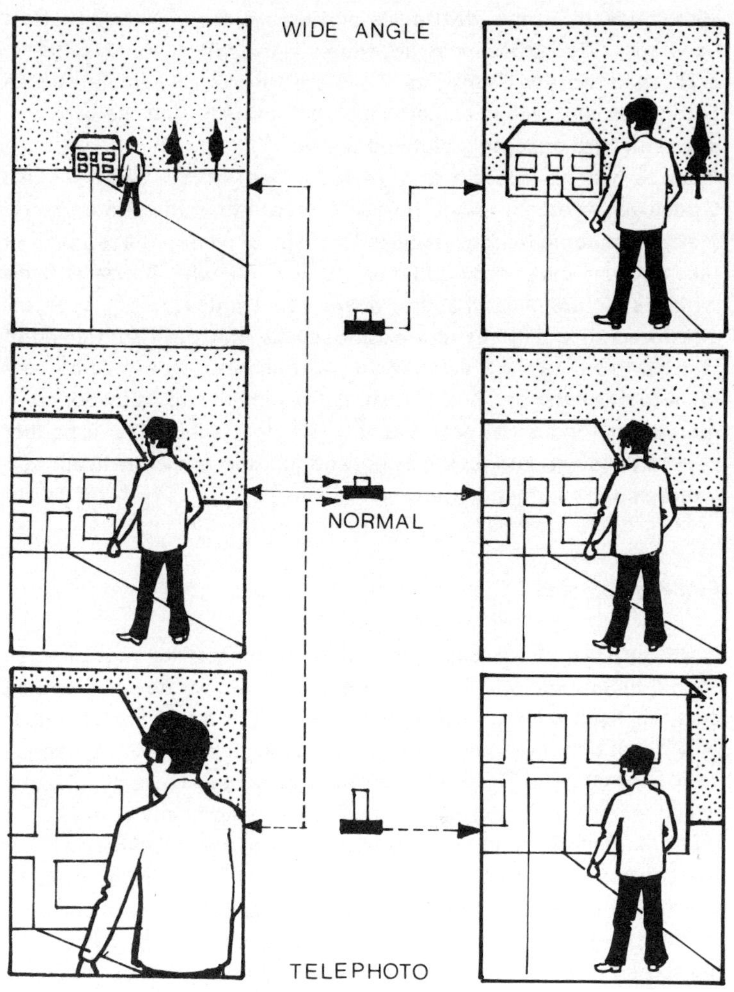

Interchangeable lenses (or a zoom lens) offer great possibilities when picturing places. When you remain in the same place, increasing focal length enlarges the whole scene at the same rate. If you move to keep your foreground the same size, then the different focal lengths change the relationship.

Perfect pictures are carefully considered compositions where mass balances mass, and light areas balance light areas. The emphasis is placed exactly in the ideal place and figures are introduced where necessary. The exposure is absolutely right, with enough detail in both shadows and highlights. They are the sort of pictures which tend to do very well in camera club competitions, and they are very satisfying and absorbing pictures to take.

Pictures with a purpose are not perfect compositions, but they make a positive statement about their subject, or rather the photographer makes a statement in the picture. This type of picture is absorbing to take because the photographer has to work out what he wants to do with the picture, and what sort of story he wants it to tell. They are also interesting pictures to look at because they have something of interest to say to the viewer. Most pictures taken by keen amateurs fall into this category, and almost all the pictures taken by the commercial and industrial professional. The right subject for a perfect picture does not crop up too often, and this sort of picture keeps you interested in the meantime.

Finding subjects

If you have a pet obsession, then finding subjects for your pictures should be no problem. Pictures of stained glass windows or vintage cars will soon pile up in your collection. But if photography is your only obsession, then you have to find subjects on which to practise your photography. There are two ways of setting yourself subjects, which will develop your picture-taking eye, your ability to develop a theme in pictures, and produce some nice pictures on the way.

Set themes are probably the simplest way of producing a situation where pictures can be found fairly easily, and little forward planning is needed. Simply load your camera with film and photograph – rainy days, reflections, shoppers, the motor car, your house, people at work, trees, concrete, roads, glass. The list is almost endless. By setting a theme, you cut down the number of pictures which you could take, but looking for a specific type of picture makes them easier to find. It narrows down the field of possible pictures.

Once you feel confident in your ability to tackle this sort of assignment, try loading your camera with black-and-white film and shoot one of these themes very quickly, using all the equipment you have in your gadget bag. Try the most outrageous viewpoints and tricks you can think of. Process the film and make a contact print of the negatives. Look at all the contacts. First of all, look for good pictures, and analyze why you like them. Secondly, look through the sheet of pictures looking for logical trains of thought, pictures which follow on and develop the ideas in earlier pictures in the series.

For instance, picture one is a normal lens shot of a tree; picture two is a wide-angle shot from the base of the tree looking upwards; picture three is a telephoto shot of the pattern of tracery formed by the branches; picture four is a telephoto shot of a bird sitting in the branches, and so on.

At first do not deliberately take that sort of series, because, at first, the gap between the pictures would be too large, and the train of thought would be too deliberate. But you will gradually develop a pictorial sense of connection, rather than a deliberately planned series. Once this sort of thing does start to develop as you shoot a series of pictures, then you will find that subjects of all sorts start presenting themselves to you. You are no longer walking, or driving along looking for a beautiful picture, you are looking for a specific *type* of picture which will help to develop your theme.

Picture-story taking is the second sort of exercise which can be useful. These are really a development of the 'connected' pictures which started to happen in the pictures on set themes. Often the pictures are very obvious, but it needs continuing concentration to see them. Some of the rules for planning and shooting a movie can be applied equally to still picture stories. First of all decide on a theme, it could be a visit to another town, or market day, or your local sports team, or a short holiday. Think in movie terms.

First you need an establishing shot, which shows a general view of your subject. If you can find one, a title slide is also useful — the signpost for your holiday town, or a poster advertising a sports meeting are typical examples.

After that, a medium shot selects an area of interest within the general shot. Then a close-up which focuses on a particular detail of the subject. Then a further medium shot allows you to shift the area of attention, perhaps back to a close-up. Mix in with the shots which are called in movie terms 'cut-aways', shots of signposts, spectators; pictures which are not directly concerned with the main theme, but add interest and variety to the overall story. Put it all together, and there is a picture story. It can be planned out in more detail using a story board technique, but to find out about these read *The Focalguide to Moviemaking*, *The Focalguide to Slides*, or *Visual Scripting* all published by Focal Press.

The advantage of this type of approach is that it encourages you to look for specific pictures, to analyze whether or not the pictures have the elements you need, and consciously decide either not to take the picture, or to simplify it. It makes it easier to form judgments about every element of the picture which appears in the viewfinder. From that point on, all your decisions are about viewpoint, focal length of lens, and exposure. Your aim throughout any photographic session is to make your pictures more and more simple, removing the distracting elements until all that is left is the point of the picture. Include less and less in your pictures and make them say more and more.

A secondary advantage to the picture story, is that it does result in slides which make excellent slide shows. They can be far more interesting to the casual viewer than a collection of pictures which leaps all over the place for its subject matter, and the only linking theme is that you consider them to be your 'best' pictures. Add taped music, and get the tape to change the slides if you like, and you are into audiovisual presentations. This is an entirely different facet of photography, and a very fascinating one in its own right.

Looking at other people's pictures

Look around at the use of photography in television, in the cinema, and most of all, in advertising. The very best photographers earn their bread and butter from taking advertising pictures. So the work of the top men is available for inspection at any time. Always look through colour supplements, magazines and watch the television to find pictures that you like.

Be careful to differentiate between liking a picture and liking the subject, for example, almost half the population enjoy looking at pictures of attractive girls, whether they are good pictures or not. However, when you find a picture you like, study it carefully to find out why you like it and how it was taken. Look at the focal length of the lens used, the depth of field, and the shutter speed. Is there any movement in the picture; has it been stopped by a high shutter speed or has it been allowed to blur to emphasize the speed? What was the photographer trying to say in his picture? Why has he framed it in the way he has? What do you think was the most important part of the subject from the exposure point of view? Has any artificial lighting, fill-in flash for example, been used? What type of film do you think he used and why?

Once you have decided how the picture was taken, think about the options that were open to the photographer. What would have happened, for example, if a telephoto lens had been used instead of a wide-angle one, and so on. Why was that viewpoint used? What difference would it make if the viewpoint had been moved a few feet to one side or the other? And the final question is – could I have taken the shot better myself?

Picture formats

My camera produces pictures which measure 24 × 36mm. Photographic paper is manufactured in a range of sizes, and very few of those sizes match the shape of my negatives. So, it seems surprising that the shape of a picture is never altered by most people. Whatever comes back from processing, or the shape the paper comes out of the packet, is *not* the shape the picture *has* to be. If you have a subject which would look best on a thin, wide picture, or a tall narrow one, then make it that shape. If you need a triangular print, do not hesitate to cut one.

If you use a negative-positive system and do not make your own prints, then white borders can be a problem when trimming the format. The only way round the problem is to ask for borderless prints from your photodealer, or to trim the white border off first. Then carefully trim the print to exactly the format you want, and if you like white borders, dry-mount the print onto white card, leaving a small white border round it. If you make your own prints, then you can mask them to any size or shape you want on the baseboard.

Slides can also be masked to give the format you want. Because slides are usually projected, it is even more necessary to frame the picture accurately, and doing so gives a lot of scope for improving the picture. It does mean that the slide must be remounted, and this can be done using any of the commercially available mounts. A word of warning here: although glass mounts do protect slides from finger marks and surface dirt, there is a certain amount of evidence which suggests that in the long term – 15 years or longer – slides which are mounted in glass may not last as long as slides which are open to the air.

Although the mounts can be bought commercially, the masks must be made up to fit the picture. Black paper can be used, but the edge of the paper usually looks 'hairy' when the slide is projected, and some contents of the paper may affect the life of the slide also. You may prefer to use commercial aluminium masks (thick cooking foil may work); cut it up and retape it into the required shape. Once the mask is the right size tape the pieces together then tape the mask to the perforated edge of the transparency before mounting it in the usual way. Remember that masking is one way of effectively producing a 'telephoto' shot, and it is the final stage in the quest to eliminate everything from the picture which does not directly contribute to the effect you want from the picture. In fact, masking slides is yet another way of adding impact and variety to the pictures you project.

Exposure

Exposure gives photographers ulcers. Some worry about it so much they have to give up photography. It is not difficult to understand but if you get it badly wrong you lose the picture. Worse still, you do not know about the mistake until the film has been processed. Obviously it is worth taking a bit of trouble to understand how to get it right (nearly) every time. Even simple cameras usually have some form of exposure setting, the time-honoured 'sunny' and 'cloudy-dull'. The more sophisticated the camera, the more control you have over exposure and the tricks which go with it.

No camera, even the most modern automatic exposure systems, can give accurate exposure for every picture, although they can for most. So it is necessary to understand what correct exposure is, when your camera or exposure meter may be fooled by the conditions, and what you can do to correct it.

What is exposure?

Exposure is simply making sure that the right amount of light reaches the film; not too little and not too much. However, except in the case of simple cameras, there is not just one correct setting, there are several settings which will give correct exposure. Which you choose depends on the type of picture you are taking.

There are two exposure controls on most cameras — shutter speeds and apertures (*f*-numbers).

Shutter speeds

The shutter speed is simply the length of time that the shutter remains open. For most pictures this is a tiny fraction of a second.

The longer the shutter speed, the more any movement will blur your picture – and that means movement of your camera or your subject.

With a standard lens, you can be sure of reasonably shake-free pictures at 1/60 second and shorter – if you hold your camera steady. This speed, too, is fine for people walking about. If you want to 'freeze' faster movements, you need a shorter (faster) shutter speed.

Long-focus (telephoto) lenses magnify movement, so if you double the focal length, you have to halve the shutter speed to achieve the same effect. (That is, use 1/125 second with a 105mm lens instead of 1/60 second with a 50 mm lens.)

Lens apertures

The aperture is simply a variable-sized hole formed by a diaphragm within the lens. Changing the aperture (f-number) alters the brightness of the light reaching your film. Because the f-numbers are really fractions; the larger the aperture, the smaller its f-number. The advantage of this system is that the same proportion of the light reaches the film at any given f-number whatever the lens.

Lens apertures also affect the *depth of field*: that is, they determine just how much of your subject is focused sharply. A smaller aperture gives a greater depth of field (more of the subject is in focus from front to back). If you are taking a picture of a distant view framed in the overhanging branches of a tree, you will want to use a small aperture (large f-number) to ensure that all the subject is in focus. On the other hand, if you are photographing a statue, you may want to use a large aperture (small f-number) to ensure that the background is out of focus, blurring confusing detail in the back.

Combinations

On the shutter speed scale in current use, changing from one setting to the next exactly doubles – or halves – the time; and on the aperture scale, changing from one f-number to the next exactly halves or doubles the brightness.

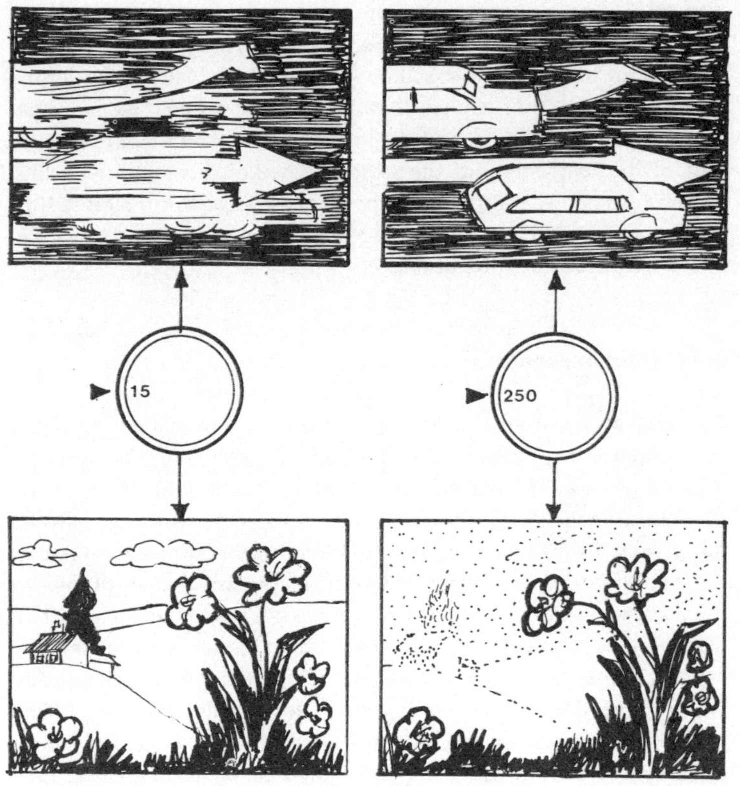

Shutter speed and aperture are important pictorial controls. Long shutter speeds picture moving subjects as an indistinct blur, while short ones 'freeze' the motion. Simultaneously, small apertures give you sharp focus from close by to the distance, while large ones concentrate on a narrow plane.

Thus, for a given exposure, you can choose one of a whole range of combinations. Imagine two sliding scales, the top one with *f*-numbers on it, and the bottom one shutter speeds. If you slide the two scales past each other until you arrive at a correct setting of aperture and film speed for a particular shutter speed, then all the other combinations are also correct. If you use a shorter shutter speed, you can compensate for it by letting more light in through a larger aperture, and vice versa. It is up to you to select the combination of shutter speed and aperture which is best suited to the subject you are photographing. This is a subject which will crop up throughout the book for specific types of subject, but the basic rule is the same one that applies throughout photography: decide what you are taking a picture of; then decide what is the most important part of that subject from the exposure setting point of view. Is it more important that no movement blurs any part of the picture (use a very fast shutter speed); or that everything in the picture is in sharp focus (use a small aperture)?

Measuring exposure

To make an accurate exposure you need to know two things; how much light there is; and how much of that light the film needs to make a picture. The meter measures how much light there is, and the film speed (printed on the film box) tells you how much light the film needs. Every time you load a film into your camera, check that the meter setting is correct. When it is correctly set up the meter measures the amount of light, and presents the result on a type of calculator which takes into account the film speed; this presents the results as the different combinations of shutter speed and aperture you can use. Cameras commonly have meters built into them, linked to the shutter speed and aperture controls. On most single-lens reflexes, the meters measure the light coming through the main lens – and so are automatically corrected for any change in lenses or accessories. Many recent electronically controlled models go further. They actually set the exposure controls for you – or set either the shutter speed or lens aperture when you select the other.

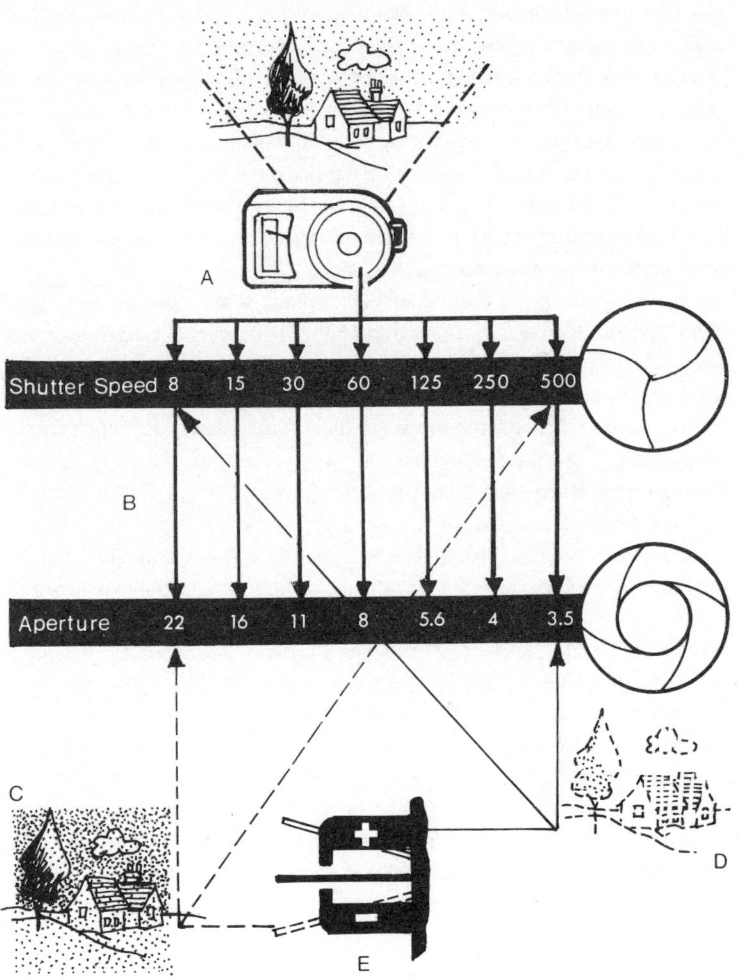

A. The exposure you need depends on the subject, lighting and film speed. B. You choose from a range of combinations. Each shutter speed having one suitable aperture. C. A faster speed or smaller aperture (without compensation) produces underexposure. D. A slower speed or wider aperture produces overexposure. E. Some internal meters show you the degree of over (+) or underexposure (−) in the viewfinder readout.

However, no device has yet been built that can do more than assume that the light it is reading from a normal subject (or possibly make pre-programmed alterations for high-contrast subjects).

'Programmed' into every type of meter is a theoretical average subject. Obviously a white card reflects more light than a black one, although the same amount of light is falling on each. Different colours and depths of colour also reflect different amounts of light. However, the meter assumes that whatever it is measuring reflects the same proportion of the light falling on it as the average subject – and that is reckoned to be about 18%.

If you are metering a subject which reflects a lot more or less light, then you must make a correction to what the meter says if you are going to get correct exposure. Before you make your reading, decide what is important about your subject – what you are photographing. Then you can make sure that you take your reading to expose that part of the picture accurately.

For example if you are photographing a view through a doorway, you are interested in the view being correctly exposed, not the door-frame. Some types of meter would give you a reading which is half-way between the two, the result is a view with washed out and weak colours and not quite enough detail in the doorway. In the same way, try to take a picture straight into the sun, there is a boat silhouetted against the sun-sparkling water. Most meters will recommend an exposure for the intense pin-points of light, and give no detail in the boat. That may be what you want, it may not; anyway, remember the effect.

Just how you measure exposure depends on the type of metering you use. But, as with cameras, the most expensive meter does not guarantee correct exposure. What it does do is allow more accurate measurement of exposure under a wider range of conditions when it is used effectively.

Separate meters

Built-in meters have now reached great heights of accuracy, and they are convenient to use, so why do most professionals still carry a separate meter with them? There are lots of reasons and habit is

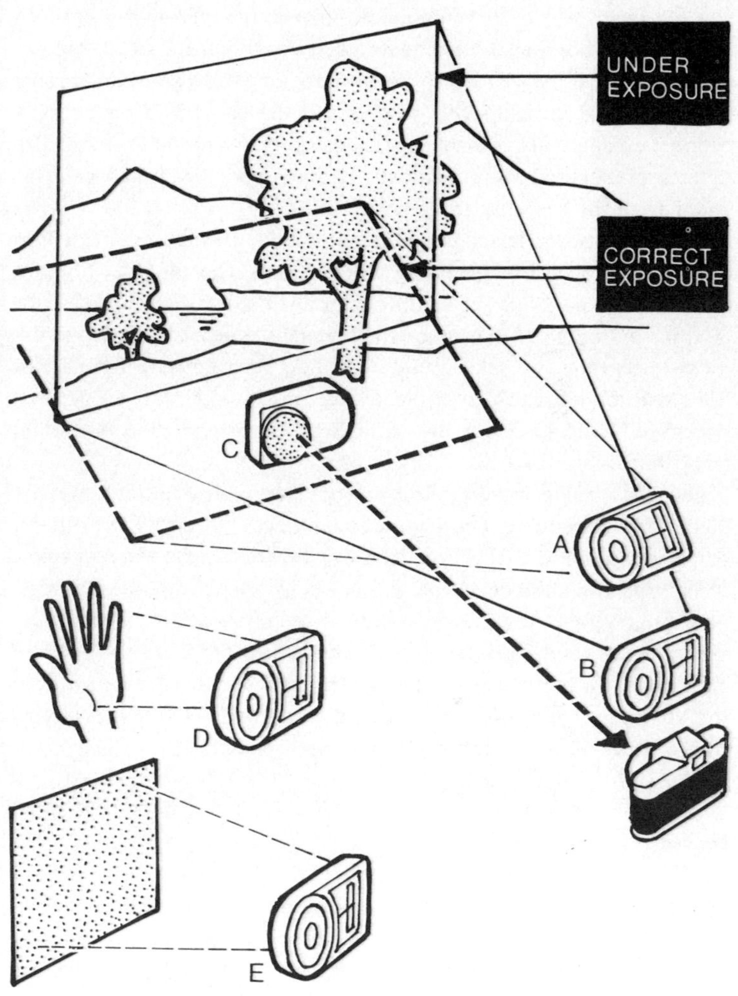

Even with a normal scene, a meter (separate or built-in) can suggest incorrect exposure. A. Tilt hand-held meters slightly downward when measuring from open scenes. B. Horizontally, the sky has too great an influence. C. Incident-light readings are a good choice for difficult scenes. D. Alternatively, take a reflected-light reading from your hand. E. An 18% reflecting grey card is an accurate substitute for an incident-light reading.

the most important of them. Meters do vary also, and if you are shooting with two or three cameras, each with a built-in meter there may be variations in the exposure between them. Separate meters can also be used away from the camera, which is useful, for example, if you are working with models and the camera is set up on a tripod, you can walk up to your subjects to take a meter reading. The most sophisticated meters can also work at very low light levels, far lower than the majority of built-in meters.

A separate meter is useful with non-standard subjects. The two classic examples are the small girl in a dark coat against a white wall, and the small girl in a white coat against a dark wall. If a subject has extremes of light and shade, decide which of the two is the most important and take a meter reading close to it. If you cannot get close to your subject (if it is a view for example), find something nearby which has about the same brightness and take a reading from that.

If you are making readings from a subject which you think may be giving a false reading, you can get a very accurate reading from the palm of your hand. Make sure that you are standing in the same sort of light as the subject. If you subject is in bright sunlight, stand in bright sunlight; if the principal part of the subject is in shade, then stand in the shade, and make your meter reading from the palm of your hand. Keep the meter as close to your hand as you can without the shadow of the meter falling across it. That reading is probably the most useful of all reflected light type readings.

Incident light metering

The other reason for using a separate meter is that they can be used to measure the amount of light falling on the subject. Because of this, they are unaffected by angle of view, and the type of subject and so give very reliable readings. Professionals depend on accurate exposure, so they tend to take several types of reading, and most usually rely on the incident light. These readings are taken, usually from the camera position, by pointing the meter at the most important source of illumination. For most pictures, that is the sun. Unless the main subject is in deep shade, you can set the reading directly

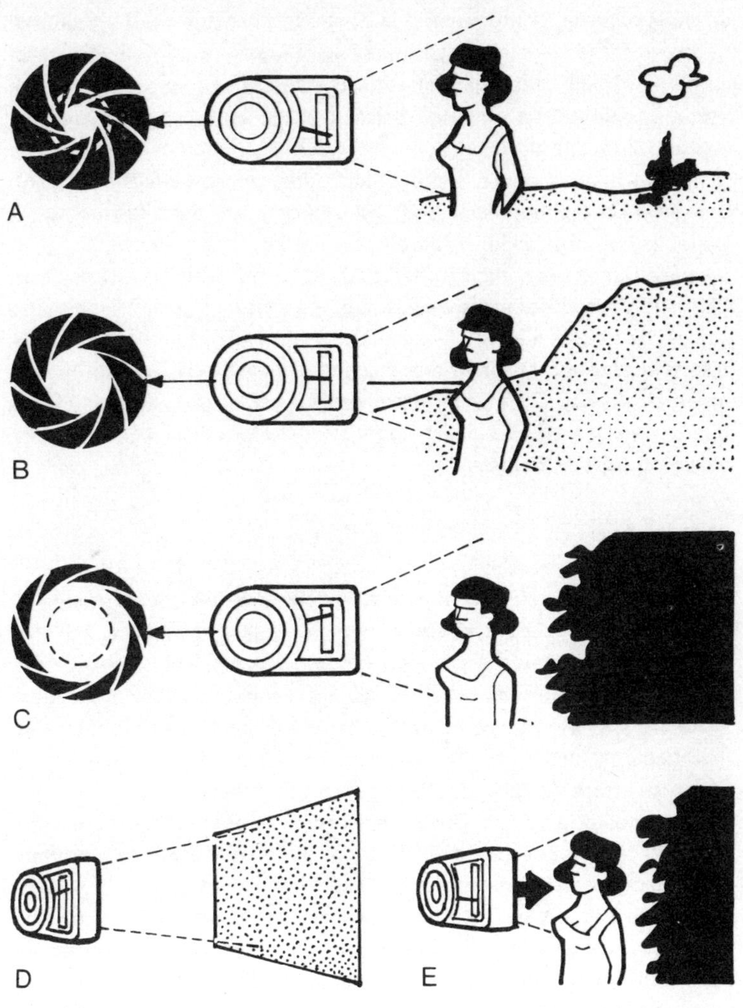

The subject and its surroundings can lead to incorrect meter readings, for satisfactory exposures, you must compensate. A. With a bright background give more exposure. B. Most subjects are more or less normal, so you can follow the meter. C. With a dark background you need to give less exposure. D. Once again, a grey card is useful, follow its readings exactly. E. When you can, go in close and meter from your main subject alone.

on your camera. If the subject is in shade, then the reading should be taken from the subject position, pointing the meter towards the *camera.* These readings *cannot* be made using a conventional meter. Incident light readings must be made using a specially made incident light meter, or a meter fitted with an incident light attachment. Normally this is a white plastic dome, but the amount of light passed by the plastic is critical, so it is difficult to make one up. A meter either can make incident light reading or it cannot.

As a system it takes a little getting used to, but with few exceptions (stained glass windows are one), it is the metering system least upset by the type of subject. If you do try incident light technique, run a test film through the camera, because it does not feel natural to make an exposure meter reading with the meter pointed away from the subject, and you need confidence before you can use any metering system accurately.

Built-in meters

The simplest sort of built-in exposure control is a separate meter in the camera body. This type do not read the light passing through the camera lens, but have lenses of their own, usually a single lens, or a series of glass dimples over the meters' sensing surface. You read exposure just as you would with a separate meter, and transfer the readings obtained to the camera controls.

Slightly more sophisticated cameras transfer the reading automatically, for example you align two needles in the meter and that sets the camera controls. Both types have the same disadvantage. Because they have their own set of lenses they may not 'see' exactly the same view as the camera lens, and objects which do not appear in the picture may affect the meter reading. The situation becomes worse when the camera accepts interchangeable lenses since the meter does not change its field to match that of the lens. Probably the last *very* expensive camera fitted with this system had one of the worst faults. If you fitted a long telephoto lens, the meter took a reading from the black lens hood. However, the system works very well with most of the subjects you will tackle when photographing places, and you will soon learn to recognize the type of subject which will fool it.

Next in order of sophistication are the 'full-frame' through-the-lens meters. They actually measure the amount of light coming through the taking lens and so alter their field of view with the taking lens. That solves many of the problems which occur with the simpler type of added-on meter. However, it can still be fooled if there are wide variations in the amounts of light and darkness within the picture. I suppose that accounts for less than 2% of the pictures most people make. When you do come across that sort of subject, then find some way of filling the frame with the main part of the subject, set the meter to that reading and then go back to your camera position. Virtually all through-the-lens meters are coupled to the lens aperture and shutter speed controls. So when the needles are aligned, or the correct LEDS alight, the camera is set for the metered exposure.

The third type goes still further towards complete control. They still read through the camera lens, so changing the lens does not affect the reading. This type, however, makes its exposure reading from a small, clearly defined area marked in the viewfinder. To use this type of meter, decide what is the most important part of the subject, and move the camera so that it lies within the marked metering area. Then set your camera. If you cannot fill the metering area with an average part of the subject, find a subject of similar brightness and set your camera on that.

There are still one or two problems with this type of meter. For example, with most through-the-lens meters light coming through the viewfinder window is reflected backwards through the viewfinder system and can affect the meter reading. It is most serious in a studio, but if you wear glasses and take a picture with the light coming from behind you and to one side, the meter can be 'fooled'.

If you have a spot-metering camera, remember that the spot you measure from must not only represent the subject, but also be a midtone. If it is not, then you have to modify your exposure in the usual way.

Virtually all current cameras use a cross between the two. The meter 'reads' the light from all over the viewing area, but gives much more prominence to the centre — or often the centre-bottom of the field. This is the best compromise for most shots. Be careful, though, in unusual conditions. If your meter measures from the bottom when you hold the camera horizontally, it may well be overinfluenced by the sky in vertical-format pictures, and go quite odd if you are photographing a snow scene. However, with a little care, they can all take accurate readings.

One way that some manufacturers simplify their cameras is to couple the meter control to just the film speed and shutter speed controls. You measure exposure through the lens with it closed down to the picture-taking aperture. This is slightly less convenient, but does avoid the possibility of exposure inaccuracies caused by worn or misaligned diaphragm linkages.

Automatic exposure control

A simple manual through-the-lens meter is probably the most convenient exposure aid for the thoughtful photographer. You can measure exposure from just the objects you want; set the camera controls, and switch off the meter. You can be quite sure that you will get accurate exposures as long as the light remains constant.

However, in new conditions, there is still a lag between seeing a picture and being sure of the exposure. That is not often critical when you are photographing places. It is, though, a nuisance on cloudy days when the light keeps changing.

To answer these problems, most camera makers now offer you the alternative of automatic-exposure cameras. Basically, these fall into two categories – those which allow you to control the combination, and those which do not.

Fully-automatic cameras set the metered exposure automatically, there is no control provided for altering or modifying that exposure. So, if the meter gives an incorrect reading, the picture will be wrongly exposed, even though you recognized a difficult subject. There is only one way to alter the exposure given by these 'sealed boxes', and that is by altering the film speed setting. For example, against-the-light pictures taken over water will always be underexposed by following the meter reading. You have to increase that exposure.

You can do this by setting a *smaller* film speed number on the meter. If the camera is calibrated in ASA, BS or ISO you *halve* the film speed to double the exposure; conversely you *double* the film

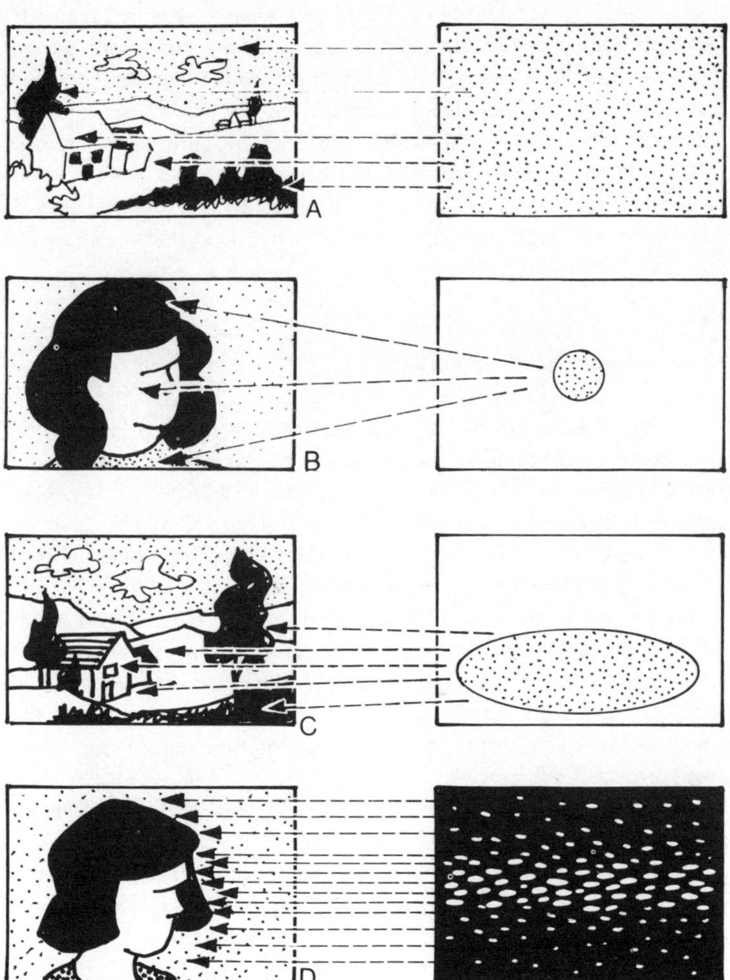

Through the lens meters vary in their sensitivity pattern. A. Some read from the entire screen area. B. Spot meters let you select a small part of the subject to read from. C. Meters may read just part of the scene, for example the bottom. D. Most read all over the scene, with extra attention to the centre. One which can measure light reflected from the shutter blind shows clearly the pattern of sensitivity.

speed to halve the exposure. If your camera is calibrated in DIN you reduce the number by three to double the exposure, or increase it by three to halve the exposure. When you alter the film speed setting on a camera always reset it as soon as you have taken the picture. If you do not, all your subsequent pictures will be incorrectly exposed. Not even this remedy is available with a cartridge-loading camera. 126 or 110 cameras (or those taking 35 mm film in 'Rapid' cassettes) are set to the correct film speed by the cartridge itself. With such a model, you must avoid unusual conditions – at least if you use transparency film.

Auto-exposure with selection

We have already seen that you can choose from a number of different combinations of shutter speed and lens aperture for each exposure. That is an important creative choice. With a match-needle camera it is usual to set either the shutter speed or the aperture first – depending on which is more critical in your picture – and to alter the other control to set the correct exposure level.
If you follow the meter's reading exactly for each picture, you might as well let the camera do the following for you. That is just what the latest generation of sophisticated automatic cameras do. In fact, they go one stage further, by setting exactly the shutter speed or aperture steplessly, rather than just choosing the nearest step in the predetermined sequence.
Most use *aperture priority* automation. With this system, you select a lens aperture, and the camera displays the equivalent meter-chosen shutter speed. When you take a picture, that is the speed the shutter gives. In practice, if you want a particular shutter speed, you simply focus on your subject and adjust the lens aperture until that speed is read out. The most basic systems actually set the exposure after the lens has stopped down. With these, you have to half press the shutter release to see what shutter speed you will get. Because of its accuracy, some sophisticated models use this metering principle, but include full-aperture simulation to display an estimate of the shutter speed that will actually be set by the automatic system.
Shutter speed priority auto exposure works the other way round;

you select a shutter speed, and the camera sets the lens aperture. Once again, you can alter the setting if the aperture is unsuitable.

The choice between the systems is a personal one. Generally, most photographers feel more secure if they can set the shutter speed; but in photographing places, the lens aperture is probably the more critical factor, because depth of field is so important. However, it is easy to learn to work with either system; and if you want the choice, you can buy a camera that allows you to select the auto-exposure mode.

Exposure override controls

Virtually all the more sophisticated cameras give you some extra control over the automatic system to cater for unusual subjects.

The simplest override is a 'backlight button'. This just increases the automatic exposure, usually by about $1\frac{1}{2}$ stops to cater for the average backlit scene. This is fine for negatives, but not really good enough for transparencies. For them, you need to alter the film speed as we discussed before. Most models, though, have an exposure compensation dial. This, in effect, modifies the film speed setting too. The compensation dial is better, though, because you are never confused as to the speed of material you have loaded.

The dial is usually labelled -2, -1, 0, $+1$, $+2$; or $\times\frac{1}{4}$, $\times\frac{1}{2}$, $\times1$, $\times2$ and $\times4$. In either case, the effect is the same. Moved away from 0 or $\times1$, the dial produces less or more exposure.

Sometimes you can decide on the amount of compensation from experience. Spotlit stage shots, for example, may need -1 (or $\times\frac{1}{2}$) to give the correct exposure; while strongly backlit scenes may require $+2$ (or $\times4$). At other times you need to make a substitute reading, a close-up reading, or (with a separate meter) an incident light reading; and then adjust the exposure compensation dial to give you that exposure for the whole scene.

In practice, if you do need to make a special reading, you are well advised to set the exposure controls manually if your camera permits. (Most automatic-exposure SLRs do allow manual exposure as well.)

The most useful (and, unfortunately the rarest) override device is a memory. With a memory, you take your exposure reading from close-up, from a substitute, with the camera pointed down, or however you feel is best. You then keep the memory switch pressed — or, often, the shutter button half pressed — to keep the exposure setting. When you take the picture, you get the remembered exposure, rather than the exposure you would get from the unusual light in that situation.

General hints

Always read the instructions supplied with any meter or camera. You will almost certainly find there are subtle ways of getting more from any metering system if you understand it properly.

Low light readings can be a problem. The most sensitive meters are expensive. If you want to take a picture under very dim lighting conditions and your meter will not give a reading, try making the reading from a piece of white card held in front of the subject. Give $2\frac{1}{2}$ stops *more* exposure than the meter suggests, if the maximum aperture of the lens will allow it. Usually you will have to multiply the exposure *time* by six.

Difficult subjects

Bright areas surrounding your subject. You will get an accurate meter reading using a spot meter; and incident light meter; an open palm reading; or by going close to your subject to take a reading. Uncorrected readings will indicate less exposure than needed. As a last resort, if you cannot use one of the correct reading techniques, give 1–2 stops more exposure than is indicated.

Dark areas surrounding your subject. You will get an accurate meter reading using the techniques listed above. As a last resort, give $1-1\frac{1}{2}$ stops less exposure than indicated.

Dark-coloured subjects. Your meter will suggest too much exposure — enough to show the subject a mid-tone. So either meter from a mid-toned substitute (such as your palm), or reduce the exposure by 1 or 2 stops, depending on how dark your subject is.

Light-coloured subjects. Conversely, your meter will suggest too little exposure – again enough to reproduce the subject as a mid-tone. So, use a substitute reading (again) or increase the exposure by 1 or 2 stops.

Sunrises and sunsets. What do you want to show? A meter reading straight into the sun will give you the correct exposure for the sun. The shadows will be completely black, with no detail. If you turn round and point your meter away from the sun, you will get the correct exposure for the foreground, but the sun will be overexposed and washed out in colour pictures. I normally use the 'turnaround' reading, but give 1 stop less exposure than that indicated, which gives me lots of colour in the sun and clouds, and a little detail in the foreground shadows. It depends on the most important part of the subject.

If you are desperate

Use the instruction sheet which comes with the film. Reading the instruction sheet is the last resort with any photographer, but the little tables included have saved many photographers from disaster when their meters have packed up.

You can also guess exposures very accurately if you remember the following rules:

Shutter speed: is the reciprocal of the film speed. Thus the shutter speed for ASA/ISO 50 film is 1/50 second.

The aperture: f16 for bright sunlight; f11 for cloudy bright weather; f8 for cloudy dull weather.

Those apertures apply for any speed of film, you merely alter the shutter speed to compensate for a different film speed, thus ASA/ISO 125 film should be exposed at a shutter speed of 1/125 second. If you want to use a slower or faster shutter speed you can do so, but you must alter the aperture setting to compensate.

The differences between the three light conditions are easy to detect. Bright sunlight leaves shadows with hard edges; cloudy bright conditions leave shadows, but with soft edges, and cloudy dull weather leaves no shadows at all.

It is very useful to make some exposures using either the sheet or by guessing your exposure. A professional, working all the time, develops a sixth sense about lighting conditions, and when they change, he notices almost immediately. As a part-time worker, you cannot hope to keep your eye as intensely tuned as that, but the exercise will help to make you aware of the way light changes. For example, as soon as the edges of shadows start to soften you should take another meter reading. Assessing the exposure you think you should be given will also help you to spot a false meter reading should you get one. Aim to reach the stage where your guess ends up within about 1 stop of your meter. Once you get used to making accurate exposures your photography becomes even more enjoyable, as you start to concentrate on getting the pictures you want, rather than the mechanics of recording anything correctly, and after all photography is fun as well.

Even with a fully reliable meter or automatic exposure camera, the rules can save you. They tell you instantly if you have set the wrong film speed, or left the compensation dial in the wrong place. Whenever you look at the settings and think 'how bright it is' or 'didn't think it was that dull', have a quick check on all the settings to be sure that they are right.

Pre-exposure checklist

1 Find your subject.
2 Decide what you are taking a picture of, for example, are you taking a picture of the square, or of the fountains in the square?
3 Now you know your subject, do you need a high shutter speed or great depth of field, for example do you want the buildings around the square to be in focus, or do you want to see the water droplets in the fountain?
4 Make your exposure meter reading from the most important mid-toned part of the subject.
5 Set the camera controls. Aperture and shutter speed first, then focus. Check the depth of field scale, or with the stop-down button, that everything you want to be sharp is sharp, and that the things you want to be out of focus are out of focus.
6 Has the light changed? No, then:
7 Frame the picture accurately.
8 Shoot.

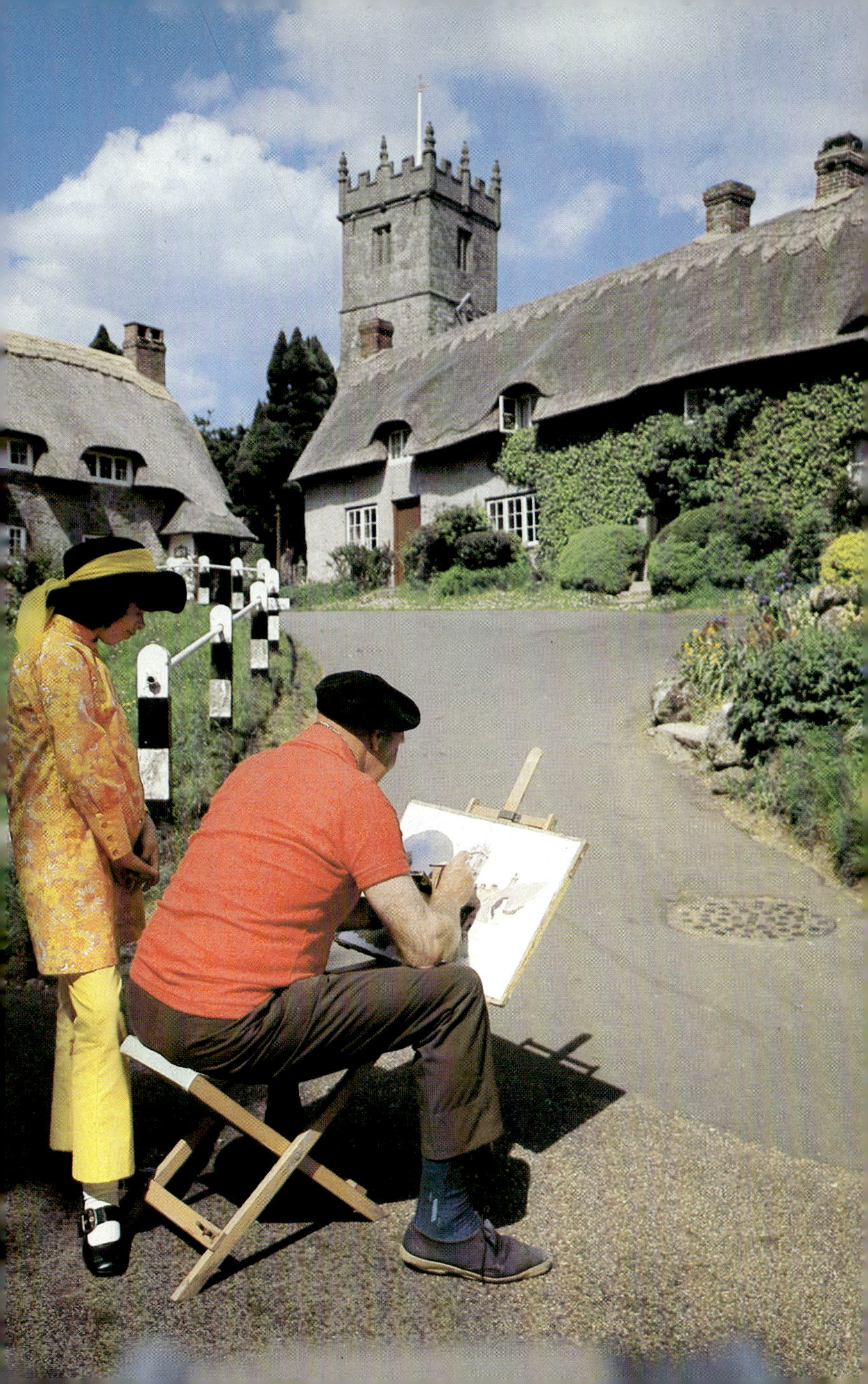

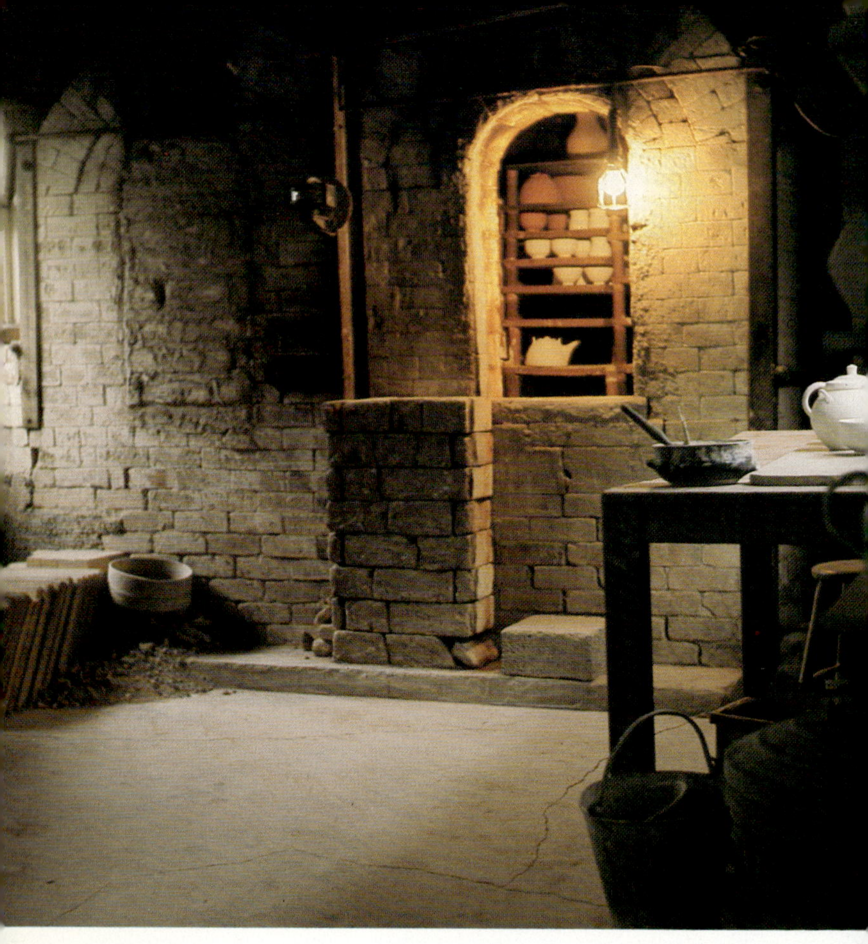

Above. Do not be afraid to mix daylight and artificial light. This would be an almost monochromatic picture without the warm glow of the electric lightbulb. *John Rocha*

Previous page. All the ingredients for a successful picture; an attractive scene, foreground interest and composition that naturally lead the eye. *John T. Pullen*

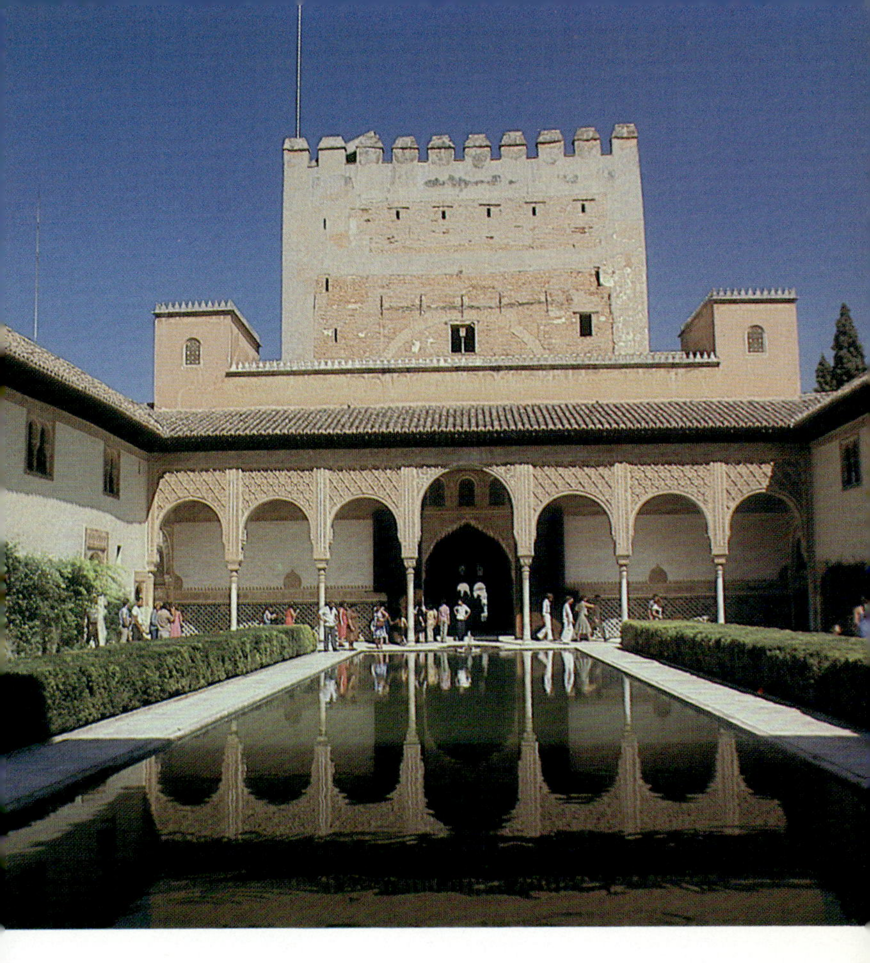

Making use of reflections helps to provide a natural balance, while a polarizing filter has darkened the sky for a more dramatic effect. *Clyde Reynolds*

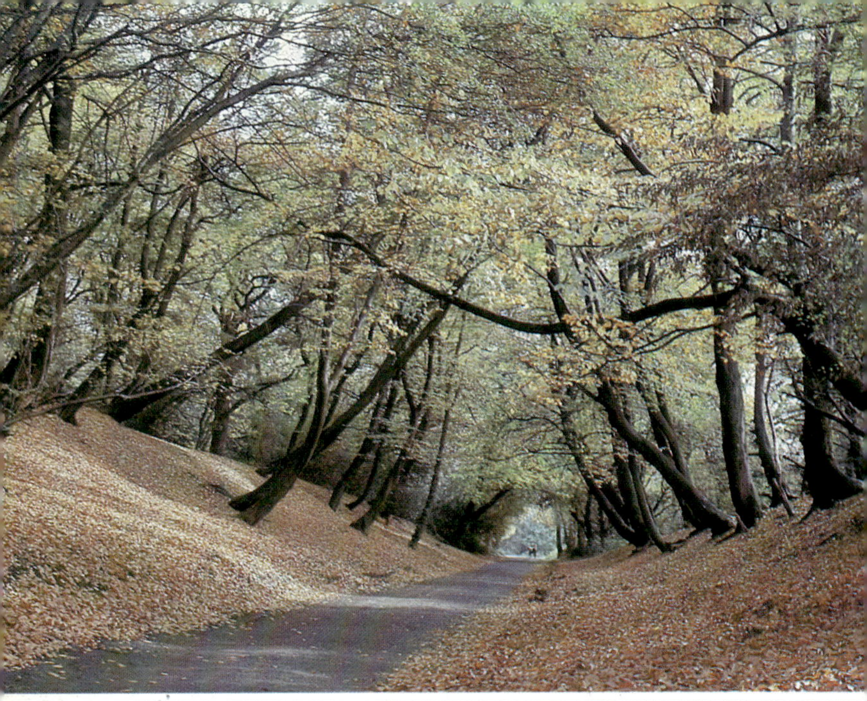

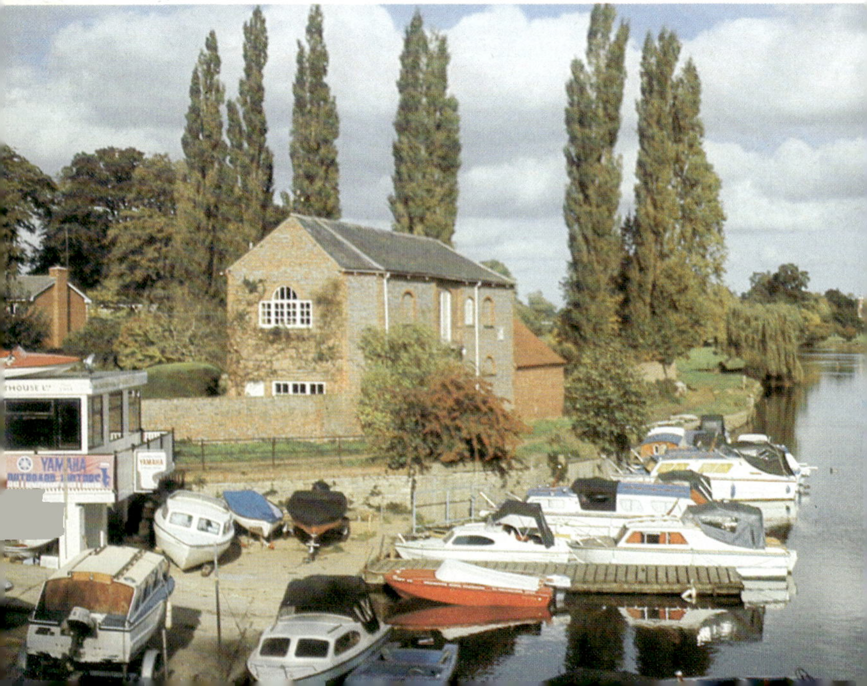

THOUSE LTD
YAMAHA
OUTBOARD & INTRODUC
YAMAHA

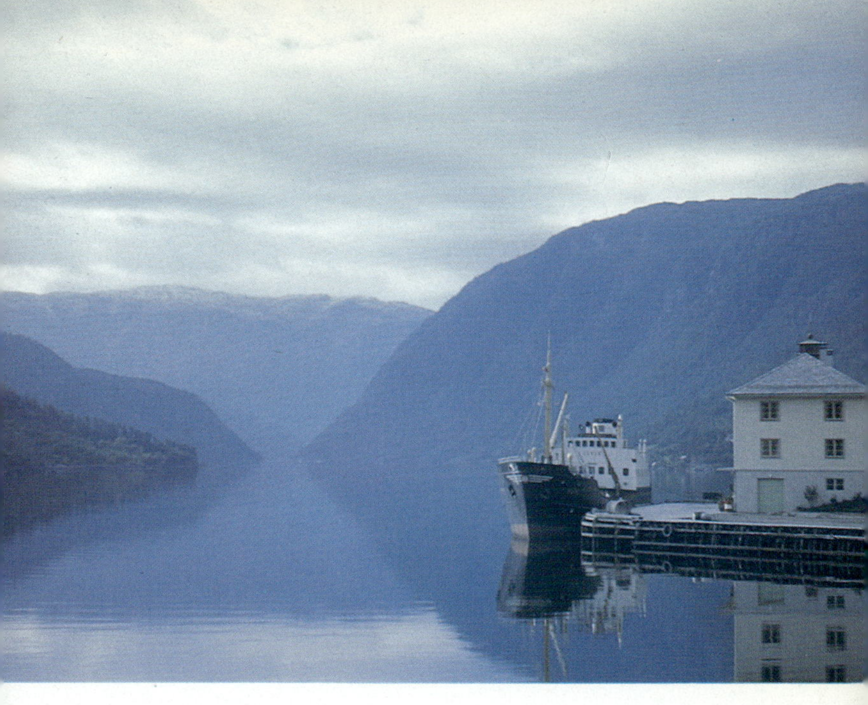

Above. A successful way to break the rules. The ship and quay have been used to oppose the natural symmetry, and the invisible ultraviolet radiation recorded by film adds colour to the scene. *P. C. Poynter*

Opposite, top. Take advantage of natural shapes. The tunnel effect of these trees and path create an impression of great depth. *P. C. Poynter*

Opposite, bottom. Without the clear stretch of water the clutter of boats would appear confusing to the eye. Use a high viewpoint to separate foreground and background planes. *Raymond Lea*

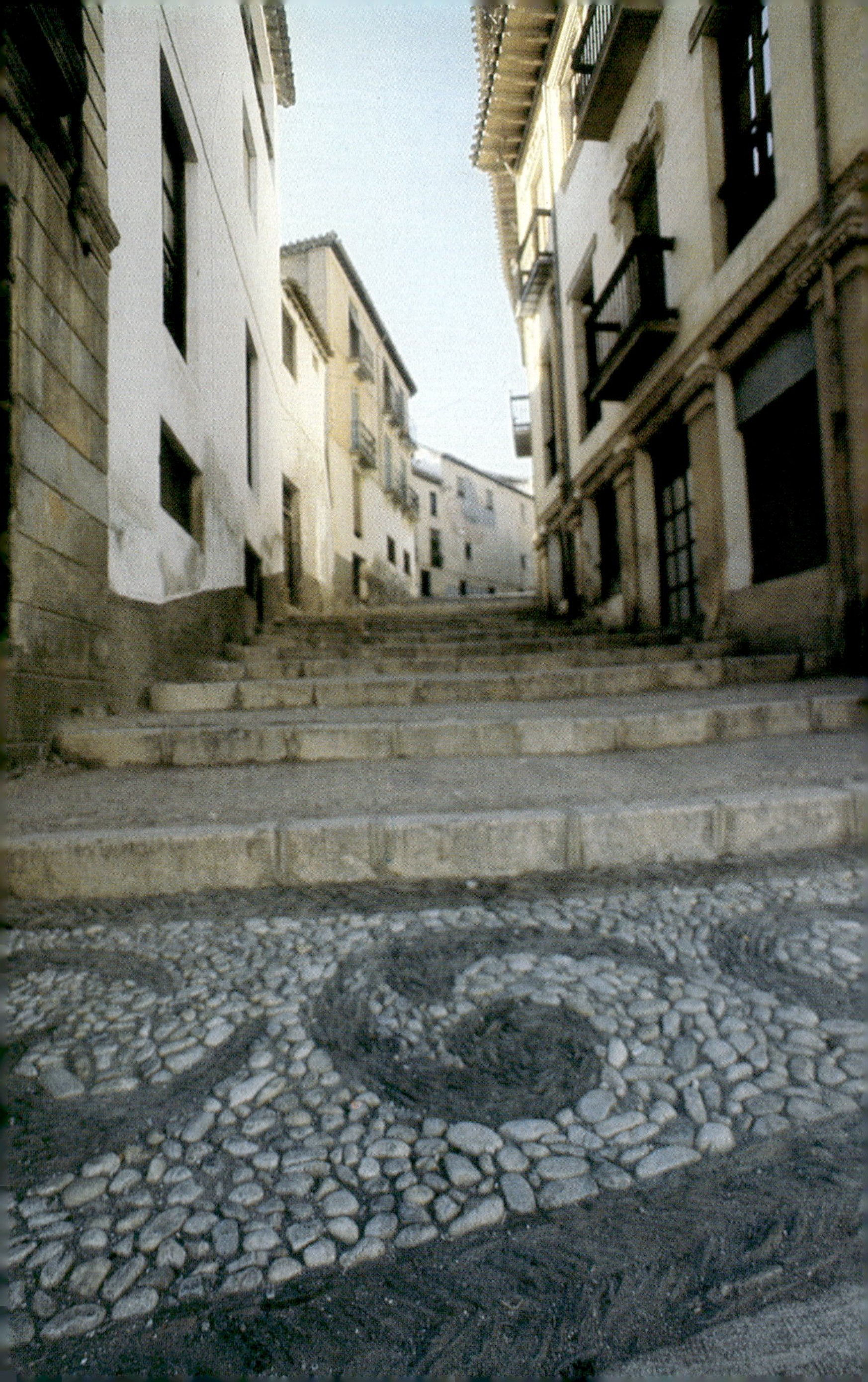

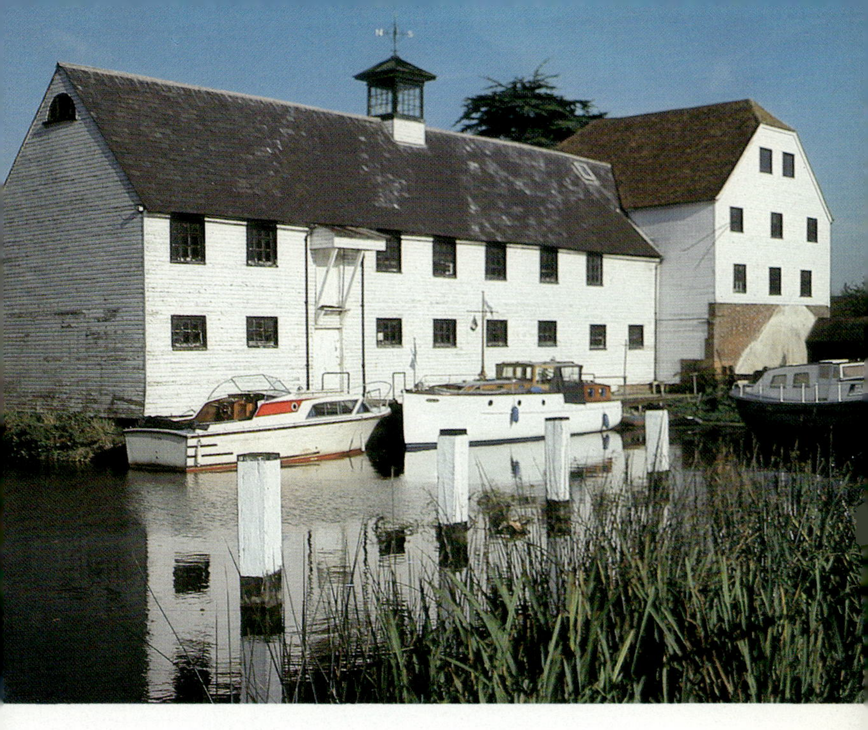

Above.   Always show the subject in relation to its environment unless a special effect is intended. *Raymond Lea*

Opposite.   Low viewpoint and wide-angle lens exaggerate the depth and steepness of this flight of steps. *Clyde Reynolds*

Overleaf.   A very striking picture is achieved by emphasizing the regular lines and shapes by choosing a suitable viewpoint and composing carefully in the camera's viewfinder. *Neville Newman*

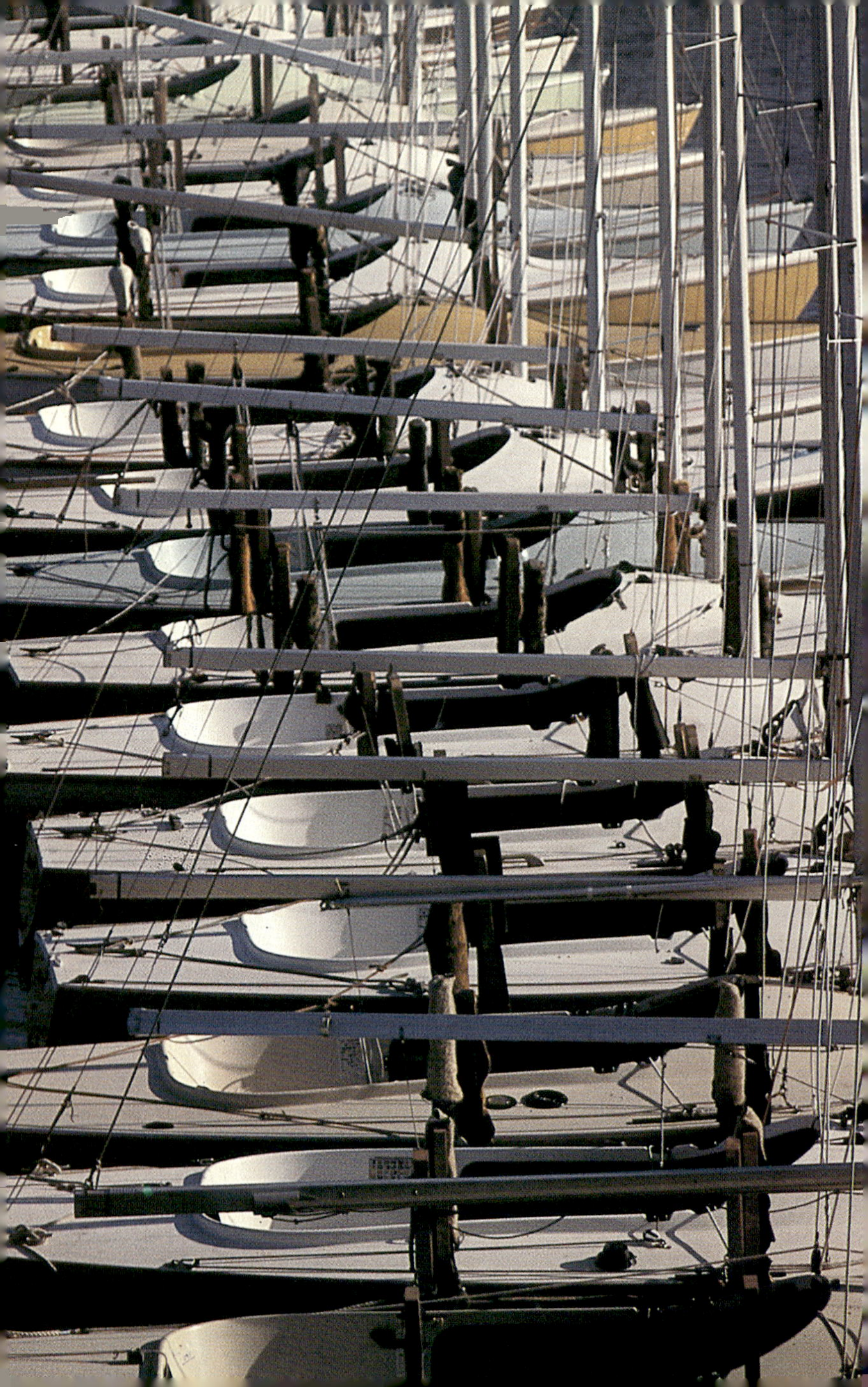

Landscapes

Landscapes are one of the most popular photographic subjects, for snaps, perfect pictures or for pictures with a purpose. Lots of people try to record a scene, or a view, with whatever sort of camera they possess. And most of them fail miserably, especially when they compare their efforts with those on picture postcards. The superior camera used by the picture postcard photographer is generally held to be the reason for the superiority of his pictures. But we know that an expensive camera does not make good pictures; a good photographer does, and it does not matter what sort of camera he is using. So what is the trick with landscape photography? Let me start by analyzing what landscape pictures are taken to show.

What is in a view?

Landscape pictures are taken to show a particularly beautiful view, they are taken to record a scene which makes you stop and look at it. But lovely views tend to disappear once you start looking at them *critically* through a viewfinder. By that I mean when you objectively search the viewfinder and say 'Does this view produce the same reaction as when I first saw it?'.

When you first look at the scene, you see it in depth, and the way your eyes see the scene is rather complex; the total angle of view is very large – about 170°, but your eye subconsciously selects the part of the picture it wishes to concentrate on, and 'fades out' the rest of the picture, while still being aware that it is there. Also your eyes scan a scene taking in a very wide angle of view and relating the various parts that you see. Normal cameras cannot match that view no matter what lens is fitted.

Your basic problem is to compress the very wide impression of a view which your eye gives you, so that your picture recreates your vision. First of all, you have an impression of depth, of the view receding from you. That is very important when recording a piece of landscape. You have to feel the land stretching away from you. So you must include something fairly close to the camera, as well as the medium and far distance. So fill the foreground of your picture. Use hedges or fences, trees, rocks or flowers, anything which will produce the contrast in size which conveys the impression of depth. You may want the foreground in or out of focus, it depends exactly what you are taking the picture of. But you almost always need something there.

You also need to compress the landscape into the small viewfinder. So you must decide on a typical feature of the landscape and compose your picture around it. There is a great temptation when you are in Holland to look around for windmills and 'Van Gogh' bridges, because that is supposed to be typical Dutch scenery. But dykes, water and wind and a wide sky are far more typical of that country's scenery. So we are looking for a picture which includes something which is typical.

This sense of depth, and of typicalness have to be combined in your picture, and the rules of composition can help. A picture always works best if it is contained within itself, if the eye is led into the scene by the strong lines in it, and there must be some point or points for the eye to rest on when it has been led into the picture, and preferably some sort of compositional stop which prevents the eyes from wandering out of the picture again. All that is fine, except that the view is there, and you cannot rearrange it. But you can move around to vary what actually appears in the picture and chose the best view.

Depth and perspective

Close by, we see the relationships between the elements of our surroundings because we have two eyes. Our brains correlate the minute differences between the two pictures to calculate distances. You can duplicate the effect photographically with a stereoscopic camera (or attachment).

At landscape distances, in practice, we use other signs to dis-

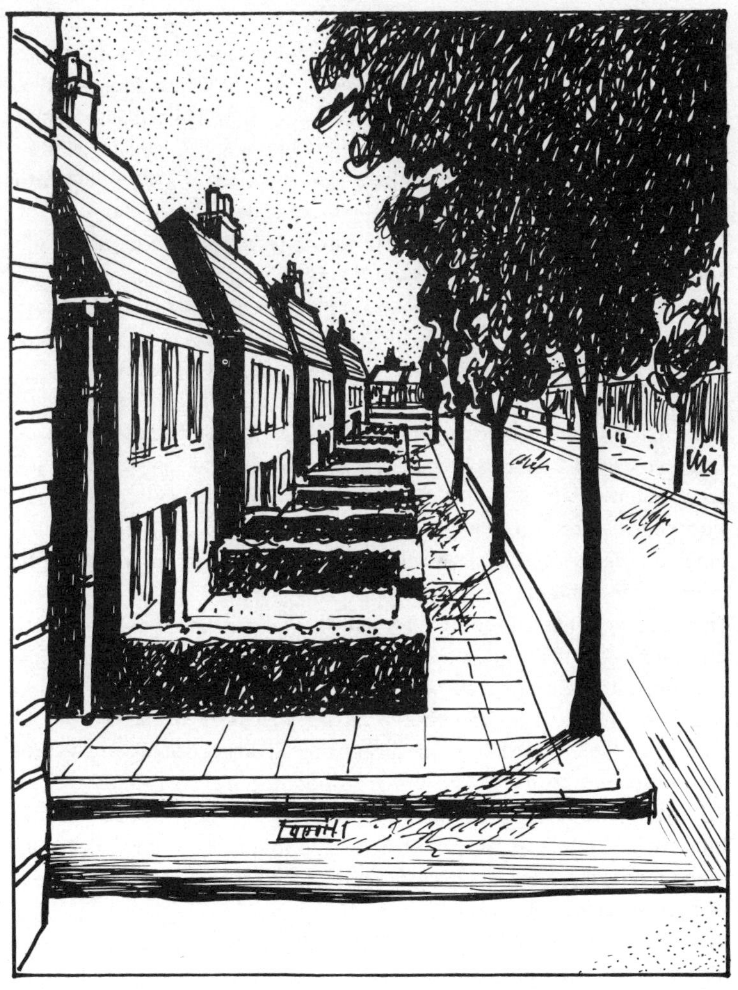

Strong lines in your subject provide a great feeling of depth.

tinguish depth. These signs are the ones you have to use in a normal photograph, however close your subject. There are three basic contributors: shape, size and contrast.

Shape we discussed a little earlier. Lines of roads, hedgerows, ploughing patterns, etc. leading to the distance give a strong feeling of depth.

Size is closely related. The reason that lines can convey depth is that they appear to converge with distance. That is, things look smaller the further away they are. Familiar objects, such as houses, trees or animals, give an instant clue to their distance. So strong is their effect that you can totally confuse your viewers if you cheat with models of familiar things carefully placed in your landscapes.

The size of texture is also important. Nearby a ploughed field appears as individual clods, in the distance, just as a speckle. That is why ultra-wide angle landscapes often appear so striking from low down, you emphasize the size of the elements of texture — the rough surface of a concrete pavement, or the individual ears in a field of barley.

Contrast is to some extent another facet of the same phenomenon. Once you look too far away to see the texture, the landscape takes on an even tone and colour. The effect, though, is emphasized considerably by the intervening atmosphere. In most of the world, for most of the time, the air is far from clean — so it scatters the light from distant objects.

This results in the phenomenon called aerial perspective. It is simply that with distance, things appear paler — and bluer. Artists have long portrayed the distance as blue, and for good reason: it is blue. To your film, in fact it is even bluer. Films are all sensitive to UV, which comes out blue in colour pictures, and white in black-and-white shots. So that faintest haze tends to become a blue veil.

So, often, you need to reduce the haze effect. You do that by absorbing the UV with a suitable filter. For a stronger effect in colour you can use a polarizing filter, and in monochrome work you can use a yellow orange, or even red filter.

When, though, you want to emphasize distance, especially when the air is clear, you may want to keep the haze. In black-and-white work, you can even emphasize it with a blue filter should you want to. Of course you cannot convey depth by just producing hazy pic-

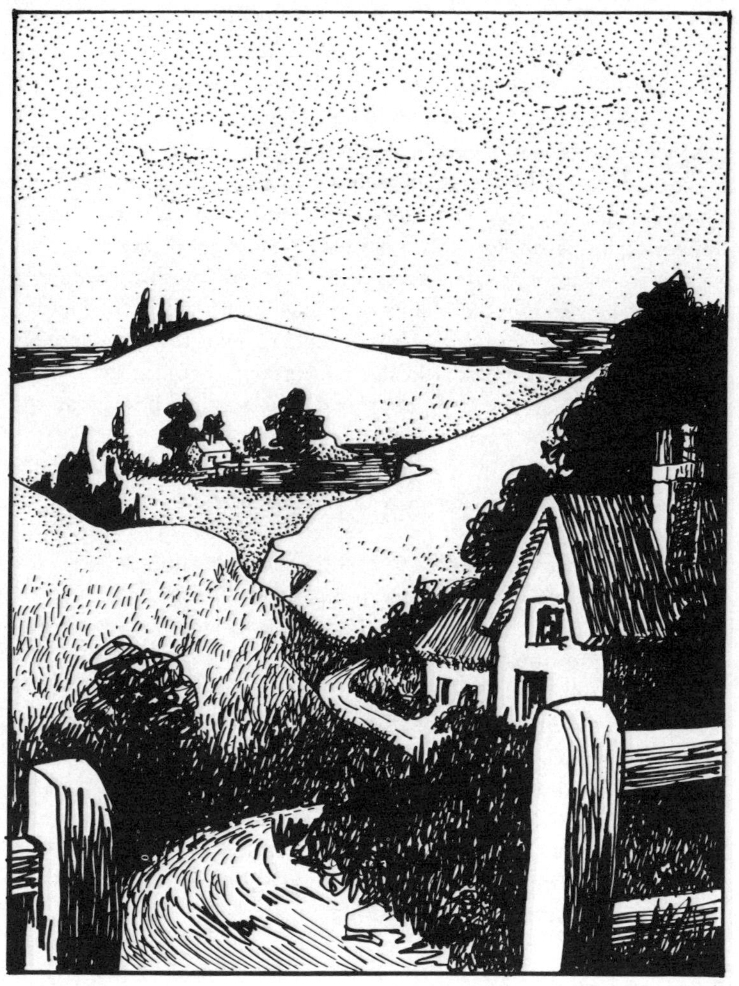

The increasing haze of distant scenes adds the third dimension to most landscapes. You can reduce it with a UV-absorbing or a polarizing filter; but sometimes you are wiser to retain the effects of depth.

tures. You need strong high contrast foreground to compare with the misty distance.

Setting up the shot

So you are out in the country and see a lovely shot of a 15th century mill against a backdrop of hills, surrounded by trees, but with a new factory built nearby. First of all walk around to find the best viewpoints, and consider the lens for each shot. With this particular location there is a perfect shot framed between the trees but there is no way you can take the picture without the factory appearing in the background. Admittedly it is a good way away, but as the trees are also well away from the mill you would need a telephoto lens to pull the mill up to a reasonable size in the picture. So abandon that shot and walk around to take the view looking another way, with the hills in the background. Look at the picture keeping an eye on the foreground and any eyesores other than the factory that might appear, like old farm machinery. Look for the most typical and uninterrupted view, hopefully with an attractive cloud-filled sky. Look for low-angle, wide-angle shots looking towards the mill sails.

Remember what you are picturing – the mill in its surrounding countryside. So you need to show that relationship. The mill is built in the middle of fields on a slight artificial incline to lift it into the wind, hence why the trees are so far away and why it is so far from the village and the hills. If you use a wide-angle lens you have to be close in to make the mill appear large in the picture. Again the close viewpoint means that the hills appear much smaller and are not noticeable in the viewfinder. With a telephoto lens you have to move much further away and the mill appears large in the picture, but it also makes the hills appear larger and closer. Maybe a little too close as the mill was originally built well away from the trees. So the best choice after all is the normal lens.

Taking the shot

Now look through the viewfinder and see what there is to see. The hills sweep down from right to left, but a clump of trees low down on the left stop the eye being carried out of the picture by the sweep of hills. If you bend down the mill stands above the line of hills and looks higher; and it appears in the right-hand side of the frame which avoids splitting the picture in two. In the foreground a field of wheat is appropriate if a little uninteresting, to increase the interest look around for some wild flowers or ask a model to walk down the path.

Now to set the exposure. The sun is bright, but it is very windy. The wind might cause camera shake so you need a fairly high shutter speed. You do not need a lot of depth of field because you are not including the nearest foreground – f8 will leave everything in focus from 5 m (15 ft) to infinity, quite enough for this picture. Now for a meter reading. Make sure to point the meter down a little. With through-the-lens metering point the camera down slightly so that the meter is not fooled by reading too much of the light reflected from the sky – 1/250 second at f8 will give the correct exposure.

Ask the model to walk and watch the progress through the view-finder and when he reaches the right place in the picture, take it. Do not stop and pose the person there. If you want to take another shot just to make sure, ask him to retrace his steps and walk along once more. A walking model is much better than a stiff, posed one. Anyone asked to stand and 'look interested' is made to feel and look awkward so always get the people in your pictures to do something.

A second shot

Briefly, let us consider the second picture. We have a 15th century mill and near to it a well-preserved village, mainly dating from the 16th century. The picture needs to show both the mill and the village it served. There is a problem because the village only appears as the tops of roofs and the church spire above the trees, but they should be clearly visible in the picture. Select a telephoto lens and walk well back from the mill with the village appearing larger in the background. Try to find two clumps of trees to form visual stops to the line of trees and village, keeping that line well up in the picture to avoid cutting the picture in two. A telephoto lens is even more difficult to hold still in this wind so increase the shutter speed to 1/500 second, opening up to *f*5.6 does not throw anything out of focus. Hang on, *squeeze* the shutter nice and slowly and we have another good shot. Because it is so windy repeat the shot in case the wind has shaken the camera first time.

Bubbling waters

Water can help enormously, it is fascinating and photogenic in itself and mirrors exacting reflections. A fast running stream can provide the key into a picture, spreading away and carrying the eye into the composition. However running water presents its own problems and offers its own rewards. Let us approach the subject logically, starting with the stream running wild down a hillside, and lead from that into the wide, smooth flowing rivers and lakes of the low plains. The fascination of running water is in its vitality, in the splash and swirl and its rapidly winding course. The photographer's problem is how to capture that effect on film. Cameras and film combine to make waves and spray look considerably less significant than they appear to the eye so unless you live near Niagara Falls or Victoria Falls you will have to make an effort to make any mountain stream look more than a rather slow little brook. For a start any stretch of running water looks more rough and broken if you look upstream. That way you see the swirls and eddies, and the white crests of the waves running over and round the rocks. Look the other way, downstream, and all you see is the almost glacial smoothness of the water as it pours down over rock, the wave below is hidden and the scene much less wild.

Be careful when choosing your viewpoint – to make the falls and spray look as big as possible you will need a low viewpoint, looking up at the water as it falls. This does not mean the most comfortable viewpoint, or the safest, so move slowly and carefully, remember that the ground underfoot may be wet and slippery. There is always a temptation to keep your eyes glued to the picture you are trying to take, but in this case, you really have got to keep glancing up as you work your way round to the camera position. Convince yourself that the best picture is not necessarily taken from the most dangerous

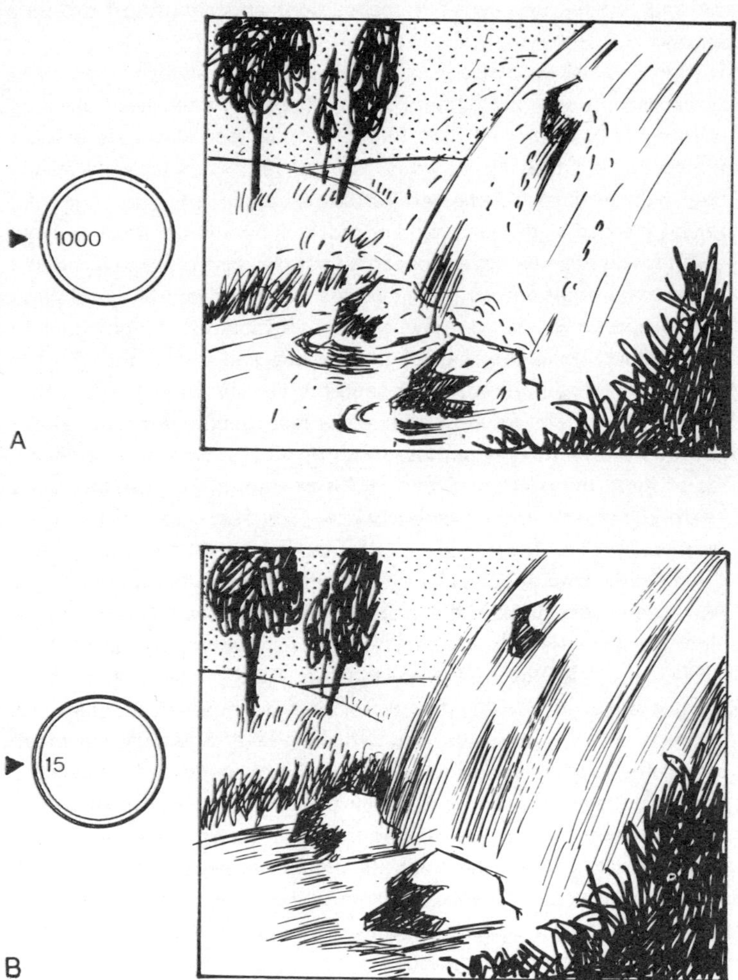

Shutter speeds are important when you have water in a landscape. A. A short exposure 'freezes' the motion to produce a crumbly effect. B. A long exposure blurs the water into a smear, which is often more attractive.

position, and always think about the effect of changing the focal length of the lens will have on your viewpoint.

A daring, wet and risky trip across wet rocks could be avoided by putting a telephoto lens on the camera and shooting from safe ground.

Having decided on a nice low viewpoint, there is always a danger of spray drifting over the camera. A UV absorbing filter fitted over the lens will help to protect that, but you should also take care to keep the spray from the camera body. You can do this by taping a plastic bag over the camera, having first cut a hole in it for the lens, and taping the bag to the lens hood once it is in position. If the bag is big enough you will still have room to adjust the controls, and if the bag is stretched tight across the viewfinder it should still be possible to see through it. Once you have taken your pictures and got back to safe ground, take the bag off the camera and thoroughly dry the body with a tissue or soft cloth, and dry the UV filter.

The choice of lens for your pictures of fast running water must depend on the picture, remember that the wide-angle lens will need a lot of foreground interest, and will make the stream recede quite sharply. If you do not immediately know which lens to use, I suggest that you mount the standard lens and try to fill the foreground. Choice of shutter speed can be quite critical with this subject. A very high speed will 'freeze' the water, showing every swirl and ripple clearly with pin-sharp accuracy. If this is the effect you want, then 1/500 or 1/1000 second is not too fast. On the other hand, a slow shutter speed will allow the water to blur, bubbles of foam will become a white shapeless blur, the waves and eddies will move during the exposure, giving the impression of speed and movement. Try for both effects, and see which one will best convey what you want to show about fast moving water. My own preference is for rocks standing sharp and clear against blurred water, and for that I would try to use 1/60 second if my foothold allows me to hold the camera still at that speed, certainly, if you go beyond 1/125 second you will start to dilute the effect.

Slowing down

Come lower down the hills and the pace of the stream slows. It is no longer so compelling as a photographic subject in its own right, but it starts to become a part of the landscape instead of one of the forces creating it. So the pictures you take in this sort of landscape are going to reflect that change. Show countryside with a stream in it, instead of the stream with a little country either side of it. The water still meanders interestingly, and used carefully it will add to your pictures. Remember the 'rules' of composition. Try to arrange the stream so that it leads into the scene. If possible, try to hide the area where it leaves the picture, behind trees or a small hillock. Trees leaning over the stream start to form useful picture frames, the flow of water has slowed up enough to allow reflections to form in the larger pools, and they can produce yet more interest and effect. Do not be afraid to include animals in your landscape pictures too, streams will always attract them and they can help to add the feeling of depth and life which you are looking for in your pictures.

At about this stage in the life of the stream you can use the reflective properties of water in another way too. You can picture reflections of sunlight as well as scenery. You have to start worrying about false meter readings once you start doing this trick, and to base your exposure of the surrounding countryside, not of the sunlight sparking on the water. This is one of the times that you have to fiddle with an automatic camera.

Still waters

Further down still and the stream has become a river, and forms lakes which reflect the view most obligingly. If the water is completely still then it forms a perfect reflection and you can make the most fascinating pictures using that perfect reflection. Do avoid the water level running across the middle of the picture, cutting it in two. Decide whether you wish to make the reflection or the subject the main part of the picture, and arrange the waterline to fall about two-thirds or one-third of the way up the picture respectively. If you do make the reflection the main part of your subject, try to avoid the real subject leading the eye out of the picture, for example by having a church spire leaving the top of the picture. Always try to keep the picture framed within itself.

If you are photographing reflections in still water, you will find that blue sky becomes a deeper blue once it is reflected, and clouds will stand out more clearly with greater contrast.

This can be a very useful effect, adding more 'weight' of colour to the bottom of the picture, and making composition easier. The effect is probably most noticeable in the classic pictures of mountain lakes, where the dark mountains contrast with snow peaks, and a clear blue sky can be reflected a deep blue, getting deeper toward the bottom of the picture. The fact that it does so is convenient, especially with the problem of filling foregrounds.

Sometimes the water can be too still, lacking life and refusing to look anything like water. A few ripples can help to bring the picture to life, and to make sure you know which way up it is supposed to be. In fact when taking pictures from boats, where foregrounds are always a very real problem, the wake of the boat is often used to fill an otherwise dead area. On lakes, you may be able to make enough of a wash by swishing your hand in the water. The old style technique was to throw a stone into the water, but I have no wish to incite people to fill up every lake, stream and pond in the photographable world with stones and boulders.

Even a good hand swishing session could upset any fishermen in the area, so make waves with caution, or they may spread further than you anticipated. If you do make some ripples, give them time to spread out over the surface, a few ripples close to the camera position and glassy stillness everywhere else looks artificial.

The problem of depth and distance is greatly eased when you have water and reflections, since the water forms the middle distance, and the far distance is taken up by whatever is being reflected. Most of the time, you will find enough interest in the shapes formed by the reflections, to happily fill the bottom part of the picture, but if you want to increase the feeling of space, you can still use trees or reeds to frame the picture. I would not do this as a matter of course, it can make the water look small and enclosed, and fight against the feeling of space and sky that attracted you to the picture in the first place. Rather I would suggest using that confining effect of reeds when you want to make the water look smaller, for example when you are photographing an ornamental lake inside formal gardens or by a stately home.

Fisheyes and the like

There are times, however, when the most assiduous search for a
viewpoint, and the cleverest hunt for a piece of typical scenery all
fail to bring that view which compresses the wide vista satisfactori-
ly. You *must* record the whole sweep of the view, but once you start
looking through the viewfinder, that idea fades rapidly.
A fisheye lens encompasses a 180° field, but it does so in all directions. The view you are aware of is 180° only in the horizontal plane.
For example, when you look at a view do you remember seeing your
feet at the same time? Your eye and the brain automatically forget
that they are there unless you specifically look for them. Use a
fisheye lens and you suddenly become aware that every picture con-
tains your feet, and because they are close to the camera they
appear very large in the picture. (In fact ultra-wide angle lenses
[13 mm – if you can afford it! 15 mm or 17 mm] are very often
much more use than fisheyes in getting everything into landscape
pictures. The effect though is quite similar.) What you actually see is
a wide-angle, but horizontal picture. Some cameras have been
produced which reproduce this sort of a field of view by using a
moderately wide-angle lens which swings during the exposure to
cover a wider angle of view. They take long, narrow pictures and
have some limited value, as do fisheye lenses.

Panoramas

There is a way of constructing the sort of panorama picture we are
talking about. You need a very firm tripod. Set up the tripod and
camera and take a series of pictures across the vista. Look through
the viewfinder each time to make sure that the picture includes the
features you want to include. Make sure that the camera swings
parallel to the horizon level. This is easier if you have a pan-and-tilt
head (one which swings both horizontally, pan; and vertically, tilt)
otherwise you will have to alter the legs until they are the correct
height to leave the camera absolutely horizontal. If the camera does
not follow the horizon accurately your finished panorama will fall
pathetically out of one end of the picture.

Start with one end of your panorama carefully framed in the view-finder. Wait for a period when the lighting will not change, for example, with clouds passing over the sun, and take your first picture. Note some landmark which marks the end of your picture and move the camera so that about one-third of your first view remains in the second picture. Then take a second picture, move the camera so that one-third of the picture remains, and take a third picture, and go on until you have covered the panorama you want.

Have the film processed and printed, or print it yourself. If you choose to print your own pictures then take great care to get the density of all the prints exactly the same, even slight differences will show up. Commercially made prints produced on an automatic printer should give prints of the same density, but this is the hardest of all tests for any printing apparatus and you may have to learn to live with some differences in density whether the prints are produced by you or by a machine.

Trim the borders off the prints if they have any. Lay the prints out on some photographic mounting board and sort them into order. You will also need a very sharp knife and a steel rule. Lay the centre print down and take the picture which lies next to it. Match the features on the edges of both prints, this will give you an overlap of about one-third of the total print. Once they are exactly matched, lay the steel rule on top of the prints, press down firmly and cut through *both* prints at once. Then take the print which matches the other side of the centre one and repeat the treatment. Carry on working out from the centre print. The outer edges of the outer prints do not need trimming. When all the prints have been trimmed, mount them onto the card taking care to butt the ends exactly together.

Mounting one section at a time is the easiest way of doing this. You may find the latex adhesive is easier to use than dry-mounting materials, although the results are not as permanent. Other techniques can be used, such as making diagonal cuts, or chamfering the edge of one print so that it lies slightly on top of the previous one. All these techniques are designed to make the join less obvious, but carefully aligned butt joints are perfectly satisfactory for normal purposes.

The reason for the massive overlap, in effect you only use the middle third of each picture, is that this minimizes the distortions which

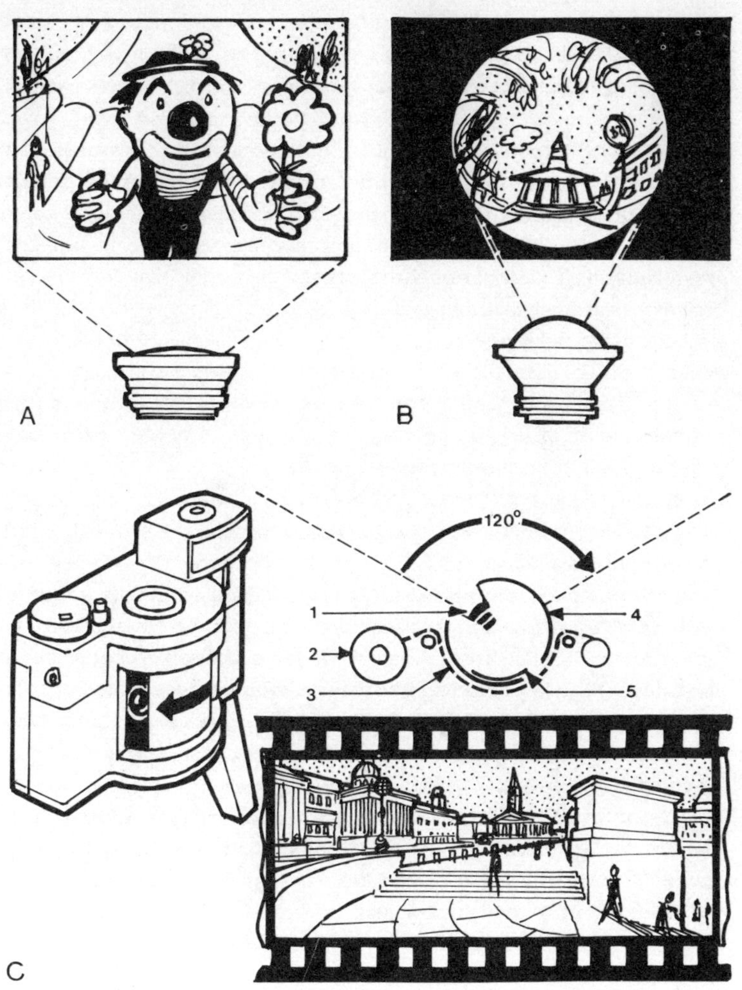

Really wide-angle shots with special lenses or cameras can add an extra dimension to your collection. A. A 16 or 17 mm fisheye fills the whole frame with a distorted image, anything really close comes out as enormous against the curving background. B. A 6, 7 or 8 mm fisheye gives you a circular image within the film area, stretching 180° or more from side to side. C. Special panoramic cameras uses a rotating lens to picture a wide sweep without distortion. 1. rotating lens 2. film cassette 3. curved film path 4. revolving drum 5. shutter.

occur at the edge of the picture, use more of the picture, and the features will not match as exactly. If you are happy to have jumps in things like fences, then you can go ahead and use more of each print.

If you find that you want to concentrate on panoramic pictures, you should consider buying a panorama head. This is a little device which goes between the tripod and your camera. It includes a spirit level to ensure accurate horizontality, and allows you to rotate the camera by a fixed angle between shots.

Light, sun and seasons

All landscape photographs are lit by the sun (yes, moonlight is just reflected sunlight). The light though, changes in angle and quality from hour to hour and from week to week.

Classically beautiful landscapes very often benefit from strong sunlight. It produces rich blacks, bright highlights and saturated colours. Every feature stands out in its own right. When the composition is right — and we have already decided what it is going to be — all that matters is the direction of the light, as we soon see.

What about the glowering Welsh mountains, though? A heavy overcast day with a livid overall light may be much more satisfactory. Or perhaps the beauty of a New England valley can best be portrayed with the soft dewy mist of an early spring morning. Whenever you have the possibility of choosing the light for your landscapes take it. The weather contributes immeasurably to landscapes. Clouds liven up the sky — and sometimes an exciting storm can be your main subject. Your foreground need be nothing more than a field of ruffled corn, or a wind-tossed lake.

Even when you want a sunlit landscape, rather than a stormscape, you have to think carefully about the light. The old advice to 'photograph with the sun over your shoulder' is correct more often with landscapes than with most other pictures. However, that is not saying much. Scenes often benefit from strong cross-lighting, especially in black and white, and shooting straight into the sun should also appeal on occasions. As we see in the Exposure chapter, this can require a little extra thought, but it is worthwhile in almost any landscape.

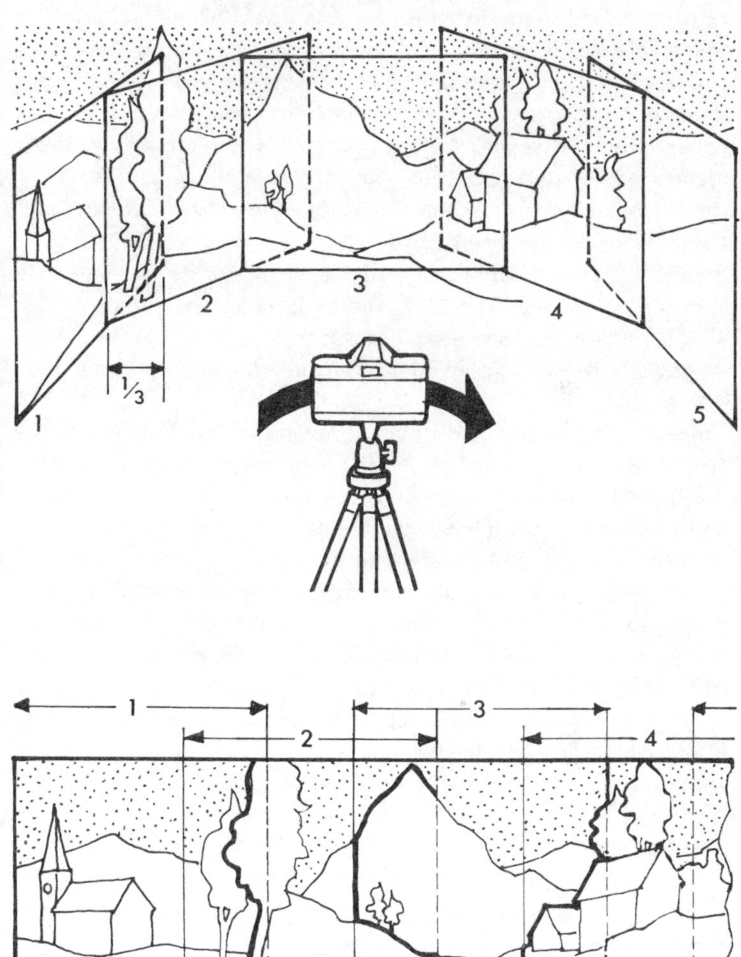

You can record a static scene as a series of shots which you later paste up to form a panorama. The camera must be mounted absolutely level, on a tripod with a swivel (pan) head. Overlap your shots by about $\frac{1}{3}$ of their width. To mount the prints, lay them out in order, and cut through both prints simultaneously at each junction. Follow lines within the subject whenever you can.

We all know that the sun rises in the east, but how often do we apply that knowledge to our landscape work. When you look at a scene, look at the way the sunlight falls on it. Could you do better if you could control the sun? Would the shot be nicer with different shadows? Or with the light slanting from the other way? It all depends on the scene, the lines of stately poplars edging many French main roads cry out for a low sun to produce long shadows. On the other hand, the brassy heat of a desert may be best portrayed with the sun directly overhead.

With just a little thought, you can predict when the sun will shine from the right place. If possible, return at the optimum time of day. Arrive a little early, and watch the scene as time passes, and the shadows move. That way you can be sure of taking the picture you want.

The sun's rays change in direction through the day, and through the year as well. Outside the equatorial zone the sun is never directly overhead, but you can still choose between a high summer sun and a low winter one. So, if the vegetation is acceptable, you can choose both the direction and the angle of the sun.

In temperate climes, though, the landscape varies dramatically with the seasons. In fact much of the joy of landscape work comes from the selection of seasonal variation. It is well worthwhile to set yourself a project of recording the seasons as reflected in your local landscape. If you are a slide-tape enthusiast, you can take a series from exactly the same viewpoint, then dissolve through it as an effective display of the year's passage.

Sunrises and sunsets

The sun coming up or going down can be an ideal subject for spectacular slides, particularly for the beginning or end of slide shows. You can bind up colourful slides with title pictures to make impressive opening and closing slides. What is needed in the picture apart from the sun? Well, clouds are always a help provided they are sufficiently broken to allow the sun to shine through. Something which has an easily identifiable shape also helps, pine trees or a windmill are good examples. Add water to reflect the colours in the sky and there is a picture which offers almost endless permutations.

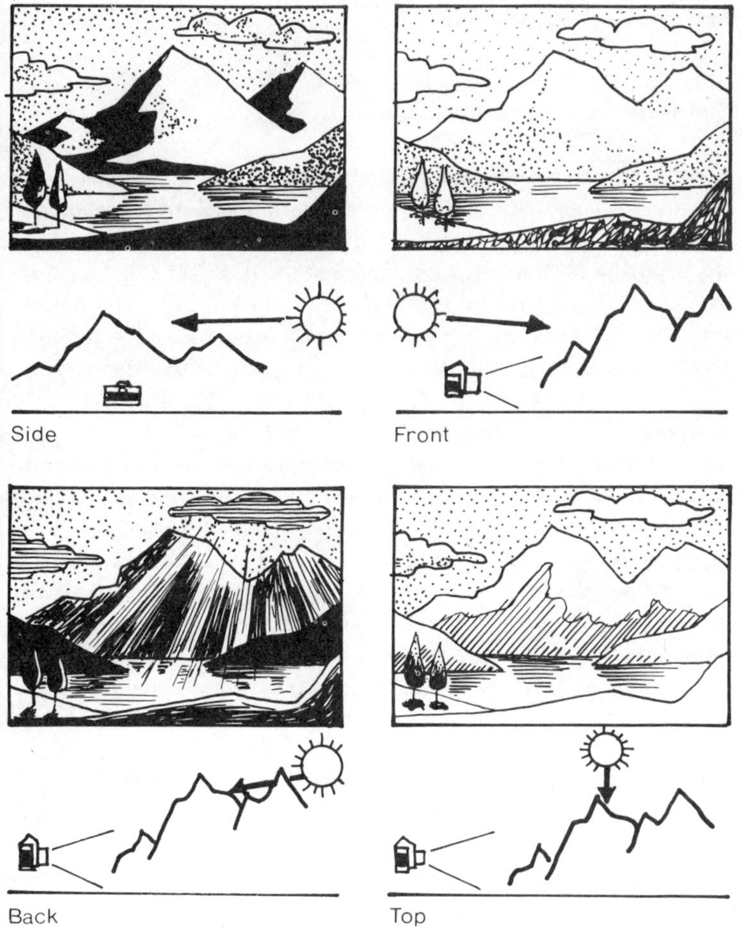

Lighting is as important in landscapes as it is in the studio. You need patience to wait for the right time of day, or even the right day of the year.

In fact the only thing which is not really needed is the sun. Pictures taken just after the sun has set can be especially effective.

One attraction of sunset pictures is that they do not need very exotic locations. I saw one recently taken by a single-handed yachtsman in mid-Atlantic, which was rather ordinary, but a picture taken from the end of a very ordinary harbour wall would have exactly the same qualities.

Exposure

How do you take them? Well one attraction is that they look difficult but are really easy. Even if you do not get the picture you originally wanted, you do end up with a nice slide. Most people worry about the exposure for this sort of picture, but the rules are still the same. Make an exposure reading for the part of the subject you are most interested in recording. If you want to record the ball of the sun then take a reading straight at the setting sun. Everything else in the picture will be underexposed giving strong silhouettes and detail only in the sky. There will be none in the foreground.

If you want detail in the shadows then make a meter reading for the shadows, but with that exposure the sun will be bright and burned out with little or no colour in the sky. For a general sunset exposure, turn round with your back to the sun and take a reading of the scenery illuminated by the sunset. It will give you an exposure half-way between the shadow reading and the reading for the sun itself. That should leave the sky bright but full of colour, but with enough detail in the shadows to please the most technical. If you have time take a series of 1 stop intervals; choose the best when the film has been processed.

When the sun is included in a picture you may see bright coloured dots or rings appear in the viewfinder. These are 'flare spots' caused by internal reflections in the lens or camera body. So far the possibility of such reflections has not been removed from even the most expensive optical systems.

But it has saved some of the most ordinary pictures. The circle type of flare can be used to form a halo round the sun, the nearer to the centre of the picture you bring the sun the more nearly the flare around it will form a circle. If the flare spots do appear there is little which can be done to remove them. Reframing the shot so that the sun does not appear in the picture and the use of a lens hood designed specifically for that lens will help. If the lens being used is more than 15 years old the flare problems may be much worse. Not only will spots and circles appear, there may also be an overall white or coloured light which makes the picture look washed out, with no depth of colour anywhere. This is called flare light or overall flare and no amount of skill can remove it. If you see it in the viewfinder, just go and look for another picture.

Building your own pictures

Clouds can add interest to the sky in a landscape picture and if there are no clouds, the answer is to put them in at the processing stage. A small stock of negatives, or transparencies with interesting cloud formations and a straight low horizon, are always valuable. The transparency can be cut carefully along the line of the horizon (sea pictures are ideal, because the horizon is straight); remount the two transparencies together. They can be accurately positioned and fastened by a piece of tape across the edges of the two pictures. In this case, mounting between glass is much the best way, since it keeps the two pieces of film in contact and prevents them flapping. The most usual combination however, is to use a nice flying bird to fill an otherwise empty sky. You do have to remember a little simple logic, though. White objects, seagulls, for example cannot mask out anything behind them. So, you cannot superimpose them on anything other than a plain white area. Transparent gannets or boobies just do not add realism. So, for stock birds, choose darker species or shoot against the light.
You can add anything dark to your transparencies — trees, maybe. All you need is a transparency of a branch silhouetted against a clear ground, bind it in with your landscape slide, and you can have silver birch leaves framing death valley – or the Antarctic wastes.
Of course, if you do your own printing, you have even more scope. Printing from negatives, you can always add darker parts to a print. The classic case is the use of a cloud negative. If your original

negative has a clear white sky, expose your print in the normal way, then change the negative for a stock cloud shot. Mask off the land (or sea) in your picture – roughly with your hand held well above the paper, or accurately with a carefully-cut mask. Then expose the sky to the clouds. Nothing could be simpler – in black-and-white or colour!

If you have a strong blue (or grey in monochrome) sky, then you have to hold it back during the first (main subject) exposure so that the paper remains white for your second (sky) exposure.

Printing from transparencies works in the opposite way. You can burn white clouds into a plain blue sky, but once you have exposed the paper to a white sky transparency the sky is white forever. In that case, you have either to mask off the sky area during the first exposure, or combine the transparencies in the enlarger carrier and make a single exposure.

Buildings

Far too much has written about 'architectural photography', describing peculiar techniques with specialist cameras, all designed to make proper photographs of buildings. You might think that it was really something special but, in fact, picturing buildings is no different from photographing landscapes, gardens or people. The basic rules are exactly the same: decide what you want to photograph; and photograph just that.

Of course, there is special equipment to help, and tricks of the trade. Like every other subject, the more sophisticated your equipment, the wider the range of pictures that you can take, and the better the quality (sharpness and correct exposure) of the picture should be. But you can make good pictures of buildings on the simplest equipment. I know an excellent collection of architectural photographs, outside and. inside, taken with a 1920s box camera bought secondhand for very little money.

What are 'buildings'? They are cathedrals and churches, castles and thatched cottages. They are also office buildings, airline terminals, hotels – and your home. All of them have one thing in common, they are designed and built by people, and intended to be used by people. The best of architectural pictures, in my opinion, are those which show people using the building. It is often difficult to avoid the people anyway, even if you want to. In most cases, it is better to relate the building to people, streets, hills, trees, rubbish tips and so forth – fashionably called its 'environment'.

Leaving buildings in their proper light

Often, on holiday or a business trip, you have no choice but to picture buildings when you are there. Whenever possible, though, a little patience and planning can make all the difference to your pictures, because different buildings need a different type of light, even different sides of the same building can show up better in different lights.

Three things affect the choice of lighting: what it is made of; which way the building faces; and what else is around it.

Obviously, you cannot actually light the building, but what you can do is to wait until the sun shines from the best direction – or until it is masked by just the right sort of cloud to soften it the way you want it.

'Lighting' always conveys the impression of arranging a series of floods and spots to produce the angles and balance you want on your model in the studio. Outdoors, though, the same principles apply. It is just that time, tide and the sun move with absolute regularity and all you can do is choose is the moment.

What is it made of?

Old buildings are often full of fine detail, delicate carving and ornaments. A strong clear sunlight across the front of the building helps to show up that detail, particularly if the building is grey, brown or dark coloured. But make sure that the shadows are not so deep as to hide part of the detail. Particularly in colour, photography tends to emphasize the blackness of shadows.

If the building material is white, then the contrast between light and shade may be too much for any film. You may lose detail in the blinding white highlights and the shadows. You have to choose a softer day. Cloudy bright is just right, with light cloud covering the sun. That produces positive but more gentle shadows to show the detail, and does not burn out the highlights.

Modern buildings, in particular, make use of very bold shapes and textures. The light and shade from strong sunlight can help to bring out these shapes. You may have to wait for the right time of day to get shadows in the right place. The pattern of shadows and shapes can produce fascinating abstract pictures in their own right. Look for these as well as for more complete 'record' shots.

72

Cross-lighting on brickwork

However skilled the bricklayer, there are always irregularities in his work. Strong cross-lighting is very unkind and shows up every tiny one. It shows were the bricks do not quite line up and areas where the courses may not be quite straight. Such light can make any piece of brick building look terrible. So, avoid it, except when portraying 'character' in old buildings, or when amassing evidence if you want to sue the builder!

Which way does the building face?

That question is not as silly as it sounds. Of course, all buildings face in all directions – since they enclose a space, but usually one side is 'prepared' for the public to see. The main entrance lobby of an office building or an art gallery, a carefully contrived view over a lake, and so on. The north face of a church, for example, is often less well detailed than the other three and can be less attractive to photograph.

If the side of the building you wish to photograph is always in shade, then 'cloudy bright' conditions will give the shade some directional light; that is the lighting to choose if you want to record some texture.

It is possible to shoot pictures of a north facing building with a clear blue sky, which gives a soft diffuse light all of its own. However, colour pictures shot in skylight appear very blue and cold. So, use a pale salmon filter ('skylight' or stronger) to improve them. You must also remember to go close in to the building to make an exposure meter reading, and point the meter slightly down, otherwise the picture will be underexposed. A deliberate overexposure of about $\frac{1}{2}$ stop may help, particularly when shooting transparencies, with buildings in deep shade.

Clouds

When buildings face the wrong way, perhaps always with one wall shaded, and too often with another brightly illuminated, you have no choice but to wait for a dull day. Clouds diffuse the sun to provide a soft even light. However, then you may find that your pictures lack impact; even that it is hard to see where one side ends and the next starts.

So, cloudy days are suitable only for subjects with their own clear shape, pattern and tones. Colour pictures are often more successful than black-and-white in such conditions.

What else is around it?

Most buildings have other buildings around them, as well as trees, large towers, pylons carrying power cables, street lighting and much else. All of them can throw a shadow across the face of the building. If you are lucky the shadow will only be there at certain times of the day. Things to the east cast a shadow in the mornings, those to the west in the afternoon. Objects to the south of the building can cause trouble for most of the day.

With luck, there is a gap in the surrounding buildings which allows a shaft of light to fall clear across the face in the early morning or late evening. It is a matter of scouting around and seeing how the land (and building) lies. If you are in a hurry and really cannot come back tomorrow, it may be possible to wait for a cloud to cross the sun and grab your picture in the brief period of shaded light. Otherwise, cloudy weather is again really the best answer. If all your days pass in a blaze of sunshine, you have to decide where the shadow gets in the way least, and take your picture then.

Constructive shadows

Shadows hide detail. That can be a great boon. Often the building you want to portray is surrounded by ugliness. If you are lucky, there will be a time when the surrounding horrors are shaded, and just your prime target sunlit. It may be that the shadows of buildings do the hiding, or clouds restrict the sun to a natural spotlight. Alternatively, if the buildings face in different directions, you just have to wait for the right sun angle.

74

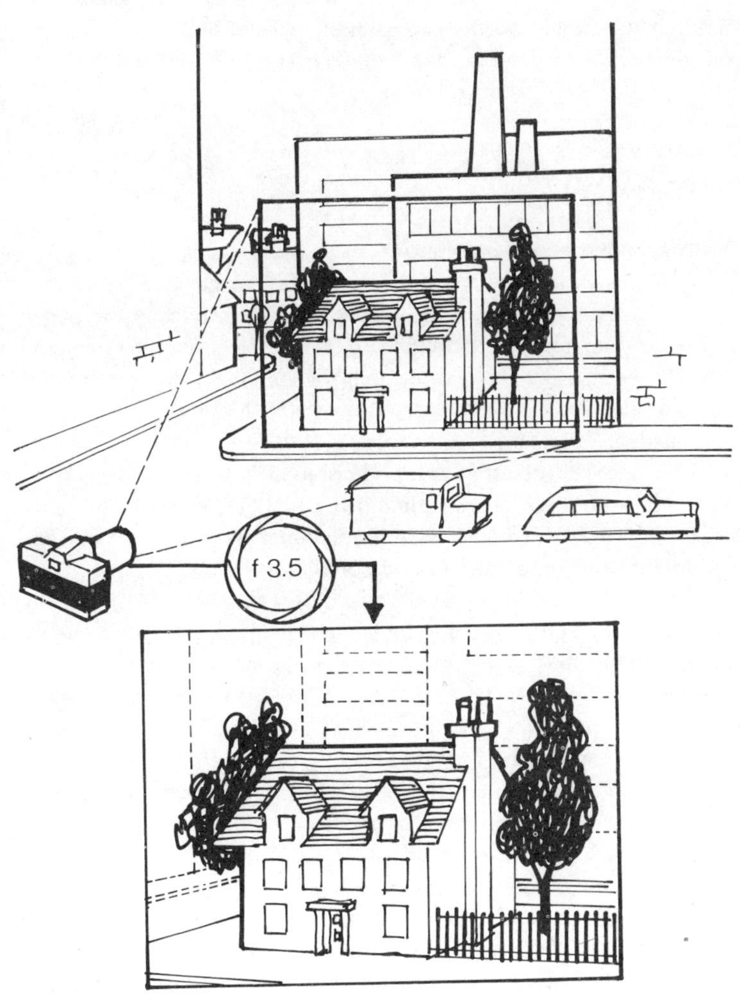

In towns, attractive buildings are often surrounded by unattractive ones. You can do much to improve your urban pictures choosing a long-focus lens to select just the portion you want; and by using a wide aperture to throw the surroundings out of focus.

Because buildings are so often arranged in streets, you are often faced with strong contrast between sunlit and shaded examples. Look on the shaded buildings as a solid mass of darkness to use to compositional advantage, leading the eye into a building, or providing a natural edge to the scene.

Do not look up!

This used to be the standard advice when taking architectural photographs. If you tilt the camera upward (to get the top of the building in the picture), the top comes out narrower than the base. So the building appears to be leaning back — away from the camera. Your eye sees exactly the same thing when you look up, but your brain corrects for it, so you are not aware of the fact when looking at a building. 'Converging verticals', as the phenomenon is called, though, can be disquieting in a photograph.

There are four ways of overcoming the problem when taking pictures: move back, or use a wider-angle lens; climb up; use special equipment; or tilt the camera and correct later.

Moving further back includes the top of the building without tilting the camera. Selecting a wider-angle lens has the same effect. When you do either, the building becomes smaller in the picture, and the foreground forms a large part. More often than not, this is being used as a car park and is not particularly attractive. That means that your final image can be made from only part of the whole frame — which implies selective printing or duplication; or masking your transparency. If you want to use the whole area, there may be other ways round the problem.

Climb up to take your picture from higher up. Perhaps there is a monument nearby with steps which you can climb. More often it means taking the picture from the upper storey of a building opposite. People are surprisingly kind when you ask permission, but take care when you open the window. Some sliding windows will not stay open on their own, and come crashing down when you let go of them. It is rarely satisfactory to take the picture through a closed window — reflections in the glass will ruin the picture. However, if you can turn all the lights off in the room and if there is only one window, it can make an interesting picture in its own right. Beware, though, of even trying with a really long-focus lens. Any lens longer than about 135 mm on a 35 mm camera will produce an appalling image through glass.

Special equipment can be expensive. The ideal machine for specialized architectural photography is a 'field camera' taking 5 × 4 in or 5 × 7 in sheet film. These cameras have *movements* which allow the lens and film to be pivoted and tilted independently of each other and give the skilled photographer considerable control of image position, depth of field and so on. But they are expensive, heavy, bulky, need a tripod – and the cost of film is fearsome.

However, the movement most used when photographing buildings is *rising front.* This allows the lens to move up and down in front of the film. The effect is to raise the camera's 'view' without tilting the camera itself. That way you get the top in without convergence. You can buy a moderately wide-angle 'shift' lens for virtually any 35 mm SLR. Such a lens offers a limited rising front facility. Using this accessory, it is possible to hold the camera horizontal and raise the lens until the foreground disappears and the top of the building is in frame.

A shift lens is surprisingly useful if you concentrate on photography in towns. I find it an especial advantage when taking horizontal-format shots, with walls all around. Unfortunately, it is also a very expensive type of lens. The reason is that the lens has to produce good definition over a much greater area than is normally asked of a 35 mm format objective. Most are either 28 mm or 35 mm focal length. The 28 mm is probably more useful, and most of the recent ones allow automatic-diaphragm operation.

One point, however, to bear in mind – shifting the lens can have a strange effect on through-the-lens exposure meters. So, always take a meter reading with the lens in its central position. Even with an automatic-exposure camera, set the controls manually if you can. If you cannot, see the Exposure chapter on ways of influencing mis-metering automatics.

Correction of convergence is possible if you do your own printing. You simply tilt the enlarging easel to compensate for the original camera tilt. When the original is projected onto the baseboard the bottom of the building is larger. Lift that end of the baseboard until the sides of the building become parallel. You have to stop down the enlarger lens enough to give enough depth of focus to make the whole print sharp. It is a technique more fully described in the *Focalguide to Enlarging.*

You never get something for nothing. So tilting the baseboard has two effects. Firstly, it means that the exposure varies across your printing paper. So you must dodge (shade) the bottom of the building a little if it is not to be overexposed.

Also, the building becomes unavoidably elongated by the process. It does also with a rising front. In practice, this has no effect on normal pictures, but does make it impossible for you to measure proportions exactly from such a photograph.

Do look up!

The alternative to all this is, of course, to go in very close to the building, put a wide-angle lens on your camera, point the camera well up into the air, and make the distortion deliberate. The pictures you can make like this are very exciting – particularly with the bold shapes of modern buildings.

Using the foreground

Everybody knows the funny picture of Aunt Edith with a tree growing out of her head, which demonstrates the importance of looking at the background when taking a picture. When photographing buildings, the foreground is even more important. If it has not been considered it can wreck an otherwise good picture. Used properly it can turn an ordinary picture into an excellent one. If you are using a wide-angle lens, the area in front of your picture becomes very important. The relative size of objects in it is much larger.

Before taking your picture, have a look round. Are there paths leading up to the building? Or flower-beds? Or ornamental paving? Or a pavement artist? Or a stall selling souvenirs or vegetables? Paths are particularly useful because they lead the eye into the pic-

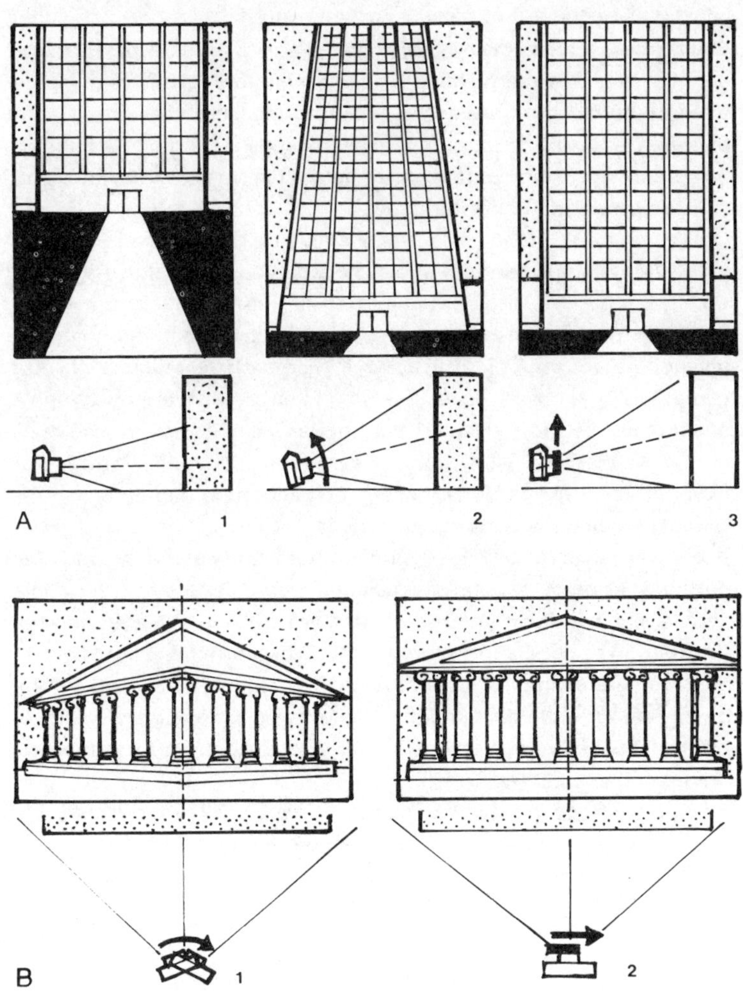

A shift lens, or rising format camera is a boon for townscapes. A. High buildings often extend beyond your picture area (1). If you tilt your camera (2), the sides then appear to converge toward the top. By raising the lens on the camera (3), you raise the picture area without tilting your camera. B. Cross shift is good for making two-shot panoramas of buildings, with horizontal lines remaining straight and parallel.

ture. If there is a patio with a particular pattern in it, then select your viewpoint to show that pattern to the best effect.

Flower-beds can be very useful, for example to hide parked cars between you and the building. The more red the flowers or plants in the foreground the greater the feeling of space and depth in your picture. Desperate photographers have been known to go and buy a pot plant which they prop or have held up in front of the camera to hide a particularly bad foreground.

Do not be afraid to bend your knees as you look for the best view-point. A low angle can hide most monstrosities, or a high angle can turn a jumble into a pleasing pattern. If you can get about half a metre (2 ft) above the heads of people walking about you, they can give depth to your picture as well. For both techniques, if your camera allows 'waist-level' viewing, you are at a considerable advantage. In fact, despite the modern emphasis on eye-level cameras, a waist-level type viewfinder is usually better for everything except photojournalistic and action photography.

Using people in the foreground does require patience and prac-tice — you have to look very carefully into the viewfinder until the pattern formed by people is pleasing. In particular the nearer people should all be walking into the picture, not walking out of it, and the distribution of people from foreground to background should be well balanced, for example, not a large crowd on the left hand side of the picture and no one on the right. It is worth developing the knack of using people in your picture — it is a good topic for the 'set themes' mentioned in Chapter 2.

If you have to go in close to a foreground subject, there are available 'half close-up lenses' which will keep the foreground sharp as well as the main subject.

Selecting a lens

When photographing buildings, there is often little or no choice of the lens you will use. The size of the building and the space available means that only one lens will fill the bill. However, if you have a choice — consider the effect of each lens.

A *wide-angle* picture with the verticals correct will emphasize the foreground to relate the building perhaps to an ornamental garden or the activity going on in front of it. It can isolate the house or make the area around it appear more spacious. It is particularly useful when photographing your own house or those of your friends. It flatters the size of the garden considerably.

A *normal lens* shot is probably the most useful for buildings. It does not produce distortions, either in the shape of the building, or in its perspective. The relationship between foreground and background remains normal, and the problem of filling the foreground is minimized.

A *telephoto lens* is chosen for one of three reasons: you have to stand too far away; to 'compress' perspective, making a building or row of buildings seem less deep than it really is; or to pick out details on the building.

Details are particularly important in churches which have interesting statuary or carvings on the face of them. The angle of lighting is very important if these are to be successful. The statues are often hidden, placed in niches, and the depth of shadow will govern the amount of detail which can be seen. Side-lighting about 45° to the face of the building is usually best for this type of picture.

More ways than one

By now you will have realized that photographing a building offers a whole range of possibilities. Each building calls for a different technique – or does it? Why not try out as many as possible on one building. For a start choose a familiar local building, and try to take twenty quite different shots. Show it in its surroundings – balanced with a strong foreground, hidden by its neighbours – show details, shapes, reflections and so on.

How many really good pictures can you take – pictures that raise a reaction from your audience? Can you take *good* pictures that local people do not recognize? This is not a pointless exercise. It allows you to begin seeing buildings from a photographer's view. When you travel, you will know just how to treat each new one.

Buildings in a landscape

This chapter has, so far, dealt with buildings which have other buildings near them. But equally, buildings can be part of a landscape, indeed the landscape may be part of the building. Many buildings have their surrounding countryside designed for them. 'Stately' homes, country clubs, schlosses and chateaux have parks and gardens designed as part of the house, put there especially to be seen from that viewpoint. The views of the house from the park and garden are designed to show the house at its best. Suburbs and the best private gardens are designed on similar lines, and that fact should contribute to the picture you take.

Remember this when you are looking closely into the viewfinder, eliminate all irrelevant detail – but the surrounding countryside may not be irrelevant. For example paths and driveways can make an excellent 'lead-in' when composing your picture. Ornamental gardens of the building, as well as making excellent picture subjects in their own right. Scale and distance will suggest which lens to use. For example, the long straight drives or 'rides' which are a feature of country houses often demand quite a long telephoto lens to 'compress' the distance to the house. Use a normal lens and the house becomes tiny in the distance.

Ornamental gardens often look best from a distant viewpoint, through a normal lens. The gardens have been laid out to give a careful symmetry and balance, which the normal lens captures with the least distortion of proportions.

Suburban gardens usually benefit from the wide-angle treatment. Plenty of foreground plants, if you are lucky a path which winds up to the house rather than being straight, and an overhanging branch can lift the routine to exotic heights. The half close-up lens can be a boon in very small gardens, and serves to increase the feeling of space dramatically.

Looking through

Views through doorways, windows and archways are always splendid for pictures. Frame them carefully so that there is a striking point

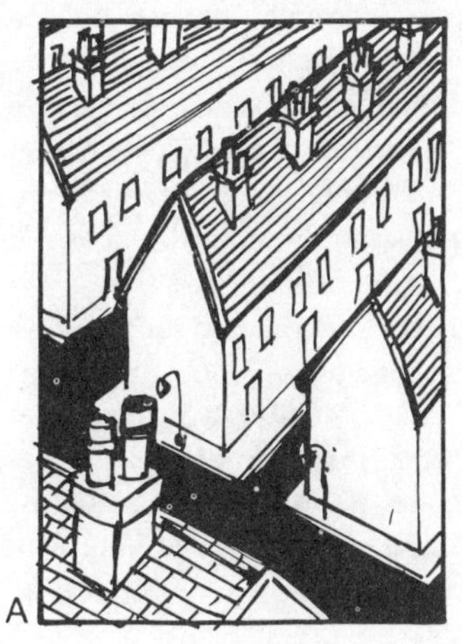

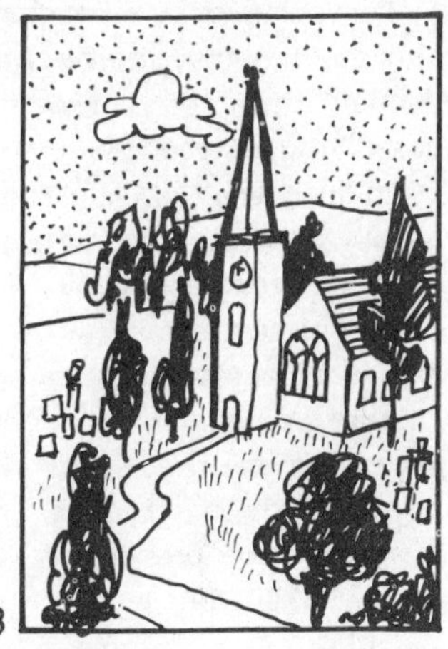

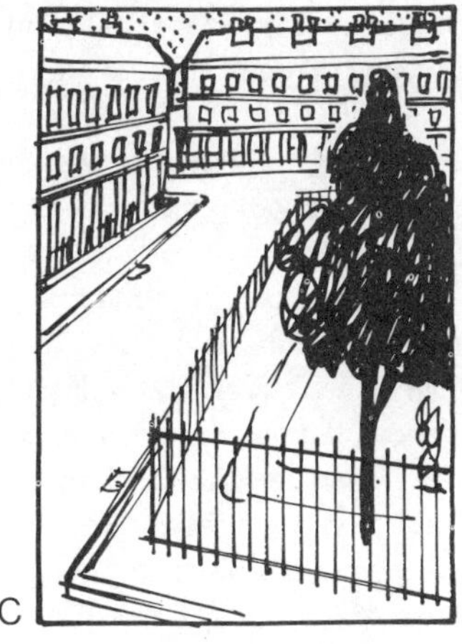

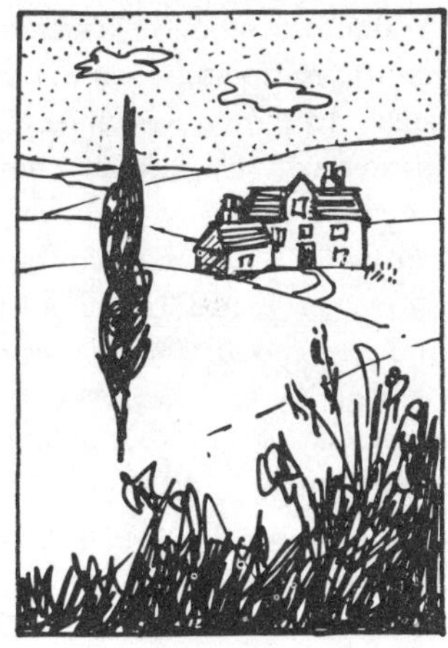

Buildings are not always best in isolation. A. A single artisan's cottage tells only part of the story. It is the serried ranks that portray industrial society. B. Step back a little from a village church, and you include its surroundings. C. Classically designed squares and terraces benefit from a distant view and wide-angle lens. D. The splendour of a country house can be enhanced by its rural isolation.

of interest in the view – a tree or statue, lake or gateway are typical. Make your exposure reading with care. Normally, expose for the outside view only. If you do not have spot metering, go up to the opening and make your meter reading directly from the outside. It is possible to expose for the shadow detail of the archway or window by making your reading close-up to this area, but the results are usually disappointing the eye is distracted by the white area in the middle where the view has 'burnt out'.

A compromise is possible by taking an exposure reading for the view and overexposing deliberately by $\frac{1}{2}$ stop for transparency material or 1 stop for negative materials. The transparency will more easily cope with the great differences in light levels. If you have your prints made by a photofinisher using fully automatic equipment, then be prepared for disappointments. If you do your own printing then detail can be retained by 'dodging' and 'burning-in' the print.

Another way of showing shadow detail is to use flash to illuminate the dark areas. If you are photographing a view through glass, be careful to position yourself off-centre to the window – looking at the view from an angle – otherwise the flash will reflect from the glass, back into the camera lens.

Using flash will produce complications, because the flash must give the same exposure that you need for the outside view. If you have a 'computer' flash that can be a help.

Make your exposure meter reading for the view. Start from the aperture you need for the view (at a suitable flash-sync speed, of course). If you can set your computer flash to that aperture, well and good – if you want the arch fully exposed. If you want shadowy details, then set the flash for a larger lens aperture (1 or 2 stops).

If you are outside the right range with the film in your camera, you have to use manual flash. Then work out the correct flash-to-subject distance for your aperture from the calculator on your flash. If it is possible to move to that distance without wrecking the view you want, do it. If that is not possible, a single layer of white handkerchief placed over the flash-head will reduce the light by about half, reducing the required distance to a quarter.

Remember, if you are using electronic flash and a camera fitted with a focal-plane shutter, you must use the shutter speed specified for

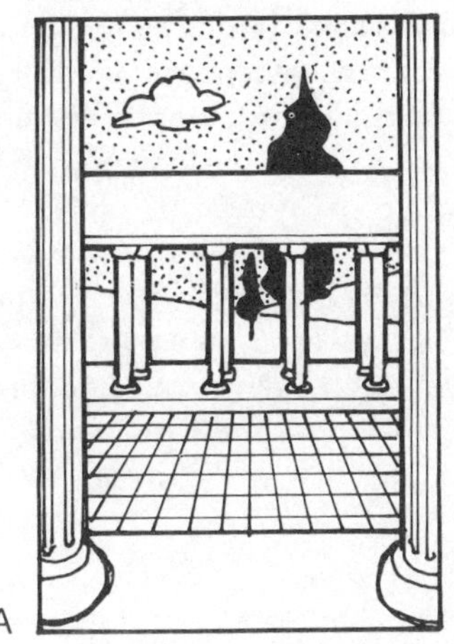 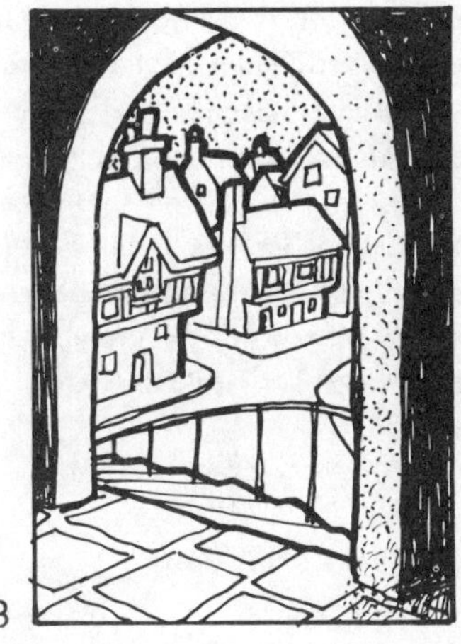

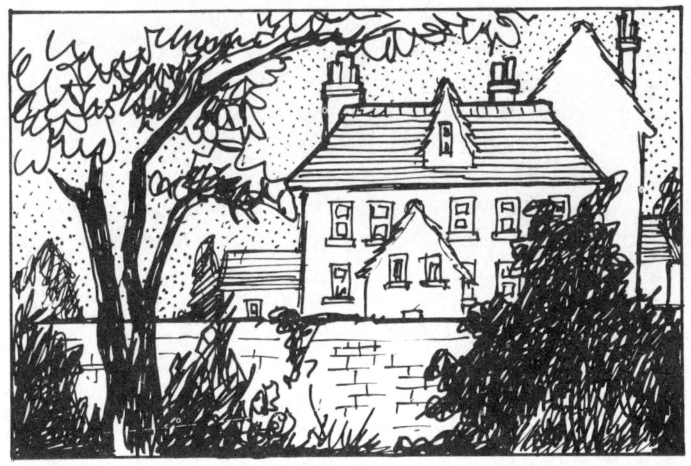

Many pictures cry out for framing, and ready-made foregrounds are often to hand. A. Foreground pillars can give a great feeling of height and spaciousness. B. Allow the top to arch in, and you have a much more closed in, confined feeling. C. Trees and shrubs are the classic rural framing agents.

flash in the camera instruction book. Set this shutter speed before you take an exposure reading from the view.

In many buildings the flashes, even of electronic flash, can be distracting and offensive to other people visiting the building – for a start it can destroy the concentration of those seriously studying. Particularly in churches the flashes of enthusiastic photographers can upset those worshipping. Flash is a useful tool for the photographer, but it must be used with consideration for others.

The use of flashguns is not allowed, or is restricted in many public buildings. This is not purely because of the distraction but also for safety reasons. If expendable flash-bulbs are used, and then thrown away, not only do they cause litter, but when they are still hot, they are a fire risk.

Buildings after dark

Highspeed films have made the photography of floodlit buildings very easy. Using 400 ASA film in Paris last year, I only found one building which needed a shutter speed of less than 1/60 second with a normal lens of f1.8. The pictures of Sacré Coeur, Paris, were shot on 200 ASA film, and the floodlighting is not very bright. The best exposure reading I could get was 1/15 second at f1.8. However, with a tight neck-strap and a convenient lamp-post to steady the camera, the hand-held exposure produced no problems. All the night-time material is considered later – once it gets dark, the subject becomes less of a determining feature in photography.

Churches and cathedrals

Ecclesiastical buildings are perhaps the most awkward of all to photograph. They tend to be long, narrow and high. Although many were built originally in open countryside, they have tended to act as centres for growth and development so many of the world's great churches are hemmed in virtually on all sides by buildings. If you are lucky, part of the building will face on to a large square and usually it is the most impressive front, as it is with, say, Notre Dame in Paris,

France, or St. Peter's in Rome, Italy. That does allow you at least to stand well back and picture the front. With other examples, such as the enormous and intricately decorated cathedral in Florence, Italy, there is no real opportunity of picturing the building as a whole structure. Wide-angle shots from close below the walls tend to make churches look strange and dumpy rather than spectacularly high and impressive.

Added to the awkward shape and confined space, are the problems of people milling about. In fact, when you are just visiting a place you are probably well advised to buy pictures (slides or postcards) of famous churches and concentrate your attention on picturing details. Look for the individualistic features of the design, like the intricate tracery of flying buttresses on the upper parts of Seville cathedral, Spain, which you can see from the top of the Geralda Tower; or the array of strange and curious gargoyles that you can find on virtually any Gothic church. This is often where your longest telephoto lens comes in.

Whether you are picking out the whole of a deeply sculptured west face or picturing a single cupid, the quality and direction of the light is particularly important. Harsh cross-lighting with its strong relief is not often suitable. A softer more diffuse day showing up shadow detail is usually better. Temples in the Far East have much in common with the older European churches. They are very intricately built with a wealth of external detail. The most striking difference, though, is in their colour. While the West's great churches are ideal subjects for a black-and-white photographer, their Eastern equivalents cry out for the most brilliant colour film.

In really hot countries most of the buildings, including religious ones, have comparatively plain outer walls, whether the white lime-washed ones of a Mexican mission or the sandy pink of an Iranian mosque. These buildings can look very impressive if you can stand well back and picture them complete. If you cannot, then you must concentrate on detail and gorgeous detail is certainly the characteristic of most mosques with their tiled doorways and tiled or gilded domes.

Some of the most decorative features of Western churches are their stained glass windows and they are something which does not show at all in a normal photograph. To see the glory of the glass the church must be lit from inside. Of course, no church has lights whose brilliance can compare to the sun. The answer is to wait for dusk. As the light fades, set up your camera on a tripod and focus it carefully on the church wall. Take a meter reading from the window and wait; keep taking meter readings of the dimly lit exterior. When the light level drops so that the two readings match then take your pictures. You may find it worth waiting even longer until the walls are underexposed by about 1 stop. That will give you a picture in which the windows glow.

Indoors

Go inside the church and your problems are magnified. Not only do you have the enormous height, but of course you cannot step back; so if you want a picture of the columns vertically, you need an extremely wide-angle lens. With a normal lens, you can pick out details, statues, tombs, and so on, and you can picture the ceiling. That is quite simple — set your camera for the floor-to-ceiling distance; set the exposure and the self-timer. Now lay your camera on the floor, lens pointing towards the ceiling. Release the self-timer mechanism and stand well back. In due time the camera will take the picture.

Unfortunately, space is not the only problem. There is often very little light and what there is tends to be highly patchy. To use a reasonably small aperture which you need to get the depth of field, your exposures are likely to run into several seconds or even minutes. If you are allowed to, use a tripod. If not, the inside of most churches provides plenty of things to rest the camera on, so that longish exposures are no problem. Brightly lit windows, though, very often are. An exposure to give you detail inside totally burns out the sky visible through the window, usually producing a rather soft flary edge. The only practical solution is to compose your pictures so that they exclude bright windows. Picturing the windows themselves is a problem only of access not of exposure. Perhaps surprisingly a meter reading taken directly from a stained glass window usually results in about the right exposure. If for some reason, perhaps you cannot get close enough, you cannot take a meter reading,

88

then try setting the normal exposure level that you would use outdoors. Try that and try opening up by 1 stop from that, depending on the colour of the glass and its cleanliness. One or the other will probably give you satisfactory pictures.

Apart from the windows, the interiors of many of the older churches of northern Europe and North America, like their exteriors are especially suited to black-and-white work. Again, more southerly churches, temples and mosques tend to use more colour inside and so need colour photography.

In religious buildings more than in any other please be careful not to upset the other people there. Always ask permission to take photographs if you can and do keep as quiet as possible. The noise of shutters can be pretty deafening and the use of motor drives or power winders is inexcusable.

Houses and smaller buildings

Much of the world's domestic architecture is very uninspired — row upon row of little boxes.

It is sometimes very difficult to make it look interesting in an attractive photograph. If you can, stand well back, use a telephoto lens and shoot through the space between other buildings. On the other hand the cramped conditions and the row of cars parked at the kerbside often confine you to the use of a wide-angle lens.

The best approach is to try and show one distinctive feature of the building or its surrounding. It may be the plastic gnomes in the garden or the marvellous decorations of the front; or it may be a more attractive and normal feature. To emphasize the gnomes you can take a shot from low down by the one sitting on a toadstool fishing in the pool using a wide-angle lens, so the little chap appears to command the whole garden with the house as a diminutive backdrop. On the other hand, to picture the colour scheme, you need a highly selective shot, probably taken with a telephoto lens to exclude the distracting colours of the neighbouring garden.

Another approach is to try and think of something to say about the building — may be that it is a cosy warm home or an extremely busy gas station. To make the place look warm and cosy, take a shot at dusk with the warm lights shining in the windows. To make the gas station look busy, not only should it be full of customers, but you need some entering and some leaving. How about a $\frac{1}{4}$ second exposure so that the moving ones are blurred. It all adds up to the message of the book — the secret of good photography is knowing what sort of picture you want to take and then taking it.

People and buildings

Most buildings were designed for people, so most building pictures look better with people in them. In fact, it is almost impossible to exclude them, but do not have them too close to the camera, otherwise you have a picture of people with a building in the background. When people are some distance away, it does not really matter whether they are facing the camera or not, nor is it too important if some of them are walking out of the scene. Once you have chosen your viewpoint, watch the scene through the viewfinder until the groups of people make a nice arrangement — then take the picture. Of course, when you include your friends or family or a model you have employed in the scene, then you probably want to picture them rather larger. If you use them carefully as a frame you can still retain the building as your main subject. Once the people become the most important part of the picture, then you are no longer picturing the place.

Of course, there are times when you really do not want any people in the picture. Sometimes you can avoid them by choosing a higher viewpoint and shooting over their heads. Sometimes you can choose your time with care — there are seldom many people in a shopping precinct at 4 am on a Sunday morning, and provided you are well away from the equator, there is plenty of light at that time on a summer morning. You can also eliminate people by giving an extremely long exposure, preferably half an hour or more, to eliminate the few who stop for a minute or so. Set up your camera firmly mounted on a tripod and reduce the light coming through the lens to a minimum. Indoors you may be able to do that just by stopping down. Outside, though, you will need a dense neutral density filter.

90

Townscapes

Most people live in groups. Photographing collections of dwellings, whether they form a hamlet or a city, involves more than just photographing a lot of individual houses. To make things simpler we will consider the whole problem under the heading 'Townscapes' because the principles are the same however large or small the community.

The basic idea is to take pictures to show the town as it is, to record the ancient and the modern, the domestic and the industrial, the administrative and the recreational, the static and the mobile, and to show how they all blend together to form a single unit. When starting from scratch, a serial approach gives you the best chance of arriving at the right pictures. Imagine that your photographs are going to illustrate a storyboard or form a slide-tape show, even if you never take a slide in your life. That helps you to develop a logical train of thought through the series of pictures. It gives an immediate clue to the sort of answers you want to the question – why am I taking this picture?

It is helpful if you start off with a caption picture if you can, a road-sign, townsign, the name over a public building such as the railway station, or the destination board of a bus maybe. Then try to get an overall view of the town. For that you need a high viewpoint, such as the top of a church tower or a hotel balcony. In mountainous regions, you can often drive up above a town and, with a telephoto lens, picture it nestling in the foothills below. Curiously this technique tends to be more flattering with modern towns. They almost always look better from above, while older towns are often more attractive from street level.

Buildings

Buildings contribute to a townscape by their individual features and by their relationships to each other and to the streets and squares of the town. From place to place in the world the buildings are different and so are their relationships. The skyscrapers of central New York are totally different from the large villas of suburban New Delhi, but pictures of the two types of building alone would do less than justice to the difference between the two areas. To show busy commercial New York needs pictures of the bustling canyons between the skyscrapers, and the placidity of the tranquil parts of New Delhi is indicated just as much by the wide tree-lined streets.

People, though, are the most important part of any town. Empty streets almost lose their meaning and the buildings become mere shells. So, for example, when you are photographing a hotel, do not just take a distant shot of the building with the correct verticals and possibly a few attractive trees around it. Try also a low wide-angle shot of a taxi in the foreground with someone getting out of it and the building tapering away into the distance. Include a few shots of luggage and porters and guests. Again, when you get inside a pin-sharp picture of large areas of beautiful carpet with geometrically placed chairs and tables may be exactly what the architect would like to see, but the same space filled with bustling holidaymakers gives a far more natural picture of the hotel.

All the problems we talked about in the last chapter return with a vengeance when you start taking pictures of townscapes. While you can often wait for an individual building to be lit in the optimum way, that is far less easy with a townscape. As the sun moves round to illuminate one building, it throws the one opposite into the shade; so when the sun is shining you often have a considerable problem with contrast. Luckily, though, in hot countries the problem is often reduced by the buildings themselves. I remember taking a transparency of a busy shopping street in Southern Portugal. It looked quite impossible — one side was lit by strong slanting sunlight; the other was in deep shadow. With no opportunity to return I decided to try anyway. I based my exposure on the sunlit buildings because to have overexposed them would have resulted in a total valueless piece of film. The result to my surprise was a quite acceptable — though not particularly exciting — transparency with plenty of detail in the not amazingly dark shadows. In fact, the predominantly white-fronted sunlit buildings had illuminated the shaded side quite well.

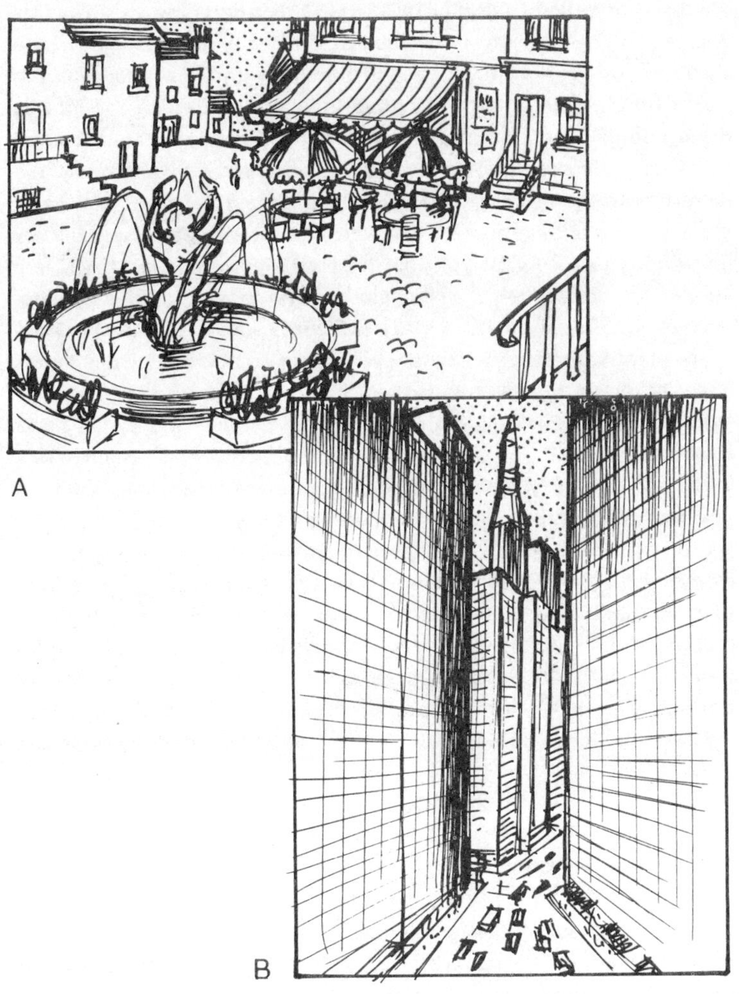

Picture shape is important. A. A horizontal picture (often called 'landscape') gives an open feeling. B. A vertical shot, complementing the feeling of an urban canyon can enhance the height and domination of the buildings.

Famous landmarks

Virtually every large town or city has its landmark — a famous building, or several famous buildings, which indicate the town as well as any nameplate could do. Of course, you need to include these in your townscapes. In fact they often make a good starting point. Before you set foot anywhere near the place you can look at other people's pictures of them. Work out what to you are the most important characteristics and try to decide how you can relate the landmark to the town. With waterside landmarks, such as the Opera House in Sydney, Australia, or the National Theatre in London, England, you may well get your best view from a boat. If you are very lucky the weather may be calm enough for you to have a reflection as well in your shot. A waterside view allows you to show the monument with the rest of the town clustered behind it. Once again, the stacked-up perspective from a telephoto lens is ideal.

When your famous building is surrounded by land and by the other buildings of the town, once again your best choice is usually a distant view in which the silhouette is instantly recognizable. Often, if you can get high enough up a wide angle view is ideal. It can show the town spreading out in all directions from its famous heart.

Some of the world's best known landmarks are bridges. They call for extra thought. Do you want to show them leading into town or leading out? Should they be impressive monuments or busy highways? What about their massive towers? Should they rise to indefinite height out of the top of your picture or should their whole majesty be included? The questions are mine, the decisions are yours.

Streets and squares

We have talked of the relationship between buildings and their streets, but do not overlook the fact that the thoroughfares themselves are an important part of the townscape. Sometimes their construction is particularly individual. For example, there are the yellow brick streets of Sophia, Bulgaria, or the cobbles found in the older parts of many European towns. On the other hand there is the rough beaten red earth that forms the main street of many a small African township. Then there is the underlying geography. What is more immediately memorable of San Francisco than its amazingly steep streets, with of course their world famous cable cars. Although it is the canals that make Venice, Italy, so famous, most tourists carry back with them an even stronger memory of the narrow paved courts and alleys with their humped bridges over the tiny canals. Of course, when in Venice you should picture its watery highways with the gondolas, waterbuses, watertaxis and boats of every description. But do take a few shots of the worn paving as well.

Roadsurfaces tend to have a much greater prominence in wide-angle shots; that is because such lenses include a lot of foreground and because they have immense depth of field so the foreground is likely to be sharp. In fact it is tempting and often worthwhile to take a number of townscapes with a wide-angle lens from very close to the ground. That way, you picture an impressive stretch of cobbles or flags leading up to the buildings. The technique is particularly impressive from the bottom of a flight of steps.

Activity on the streets

Almost everywhere in the world as well as being arteries of communication, streets are centres of commerce. In the comparatively well regulated West, most of such commerce takes place in preappointed places. Streets or squares are set aside for market stalls, and they provide endless possibilities for the creative photographer. No one, though, is going to stop and pose for you. In fact in some places photographers are beginning to be regarded as a nuisance, so you must be ready to take pictures very quickly. Take a meter reading underneath the awnings of the stalls and set your camera controls to give you a reasonable aperture and adjust the lens to give you a reasonable zone of sharp focus. For example, with a standard lens set on 3 m (10 ft) and an aperture of $f8$, your pictures will be sharp from about 2 m (7 ft) to about 6 m (20 ft).

More often, though, you are likely to use a wide-angle lens which should give you an even deeper zone of sharp focus. With a 24 or

28 mm lens on a 35 mm camera, you can compose your pictures so that you show both the stallkeeper and his wares, and with luck a customer in the process of transacting a deal. In the West we are accustomed to going to large modern shops for much of the shopping, but the market is a much more important centre for trade in countries of the Middle and Far East. The bazaar in Istanbul is typical of the sort of trading centre you can expect. It consists of mile after mile of covered arcade bordered by lock-up shop units. Trade is divided between the streets and the shops themselves. From the photographer's point of view, this arrangement suffers from considerable crowding and lack of light. The most you can normally hope to do is to record impressions on a high speed film through a wide-angle lens.

Industry

In some countries little open-fronted shops face directly onto normal open air streets. Many of them just supply the normal necessities of life, and are not especially interesting to the photographer. However, if you look in the right places you can find rows of shops full of craftsmen: silversmiths, woodcarvers, embroiderers, carpetmakers or whatever. The open fronts of these shops mean that however dingy their interior enough light normally falls on the workers for you to take very good photographs, if they do not mind you doing so. The craftsmen usually work at low tables or on the ground, so you can stand over them to take your pictures. For this sort of picture the standard lens is usually the best.
While few travellers go out of their way to visit the local steel mills, it is quite common to go on tours of more craft-orientated light industries, especially in developing countries. Examples that spring immediately to mind are potteries, vineyards, carpet works, and diamond cutters. Most of these activities take place, at least partly, in well lit small workshops. Load your camera with high speed film; mount the standard lens and you are well equipped in most cases. You should be able to use exposures of around 1/30 second at f4; that provides you with adequate depth of field and with a little judicious leaning a reasonable chance of getting sharp hand-held

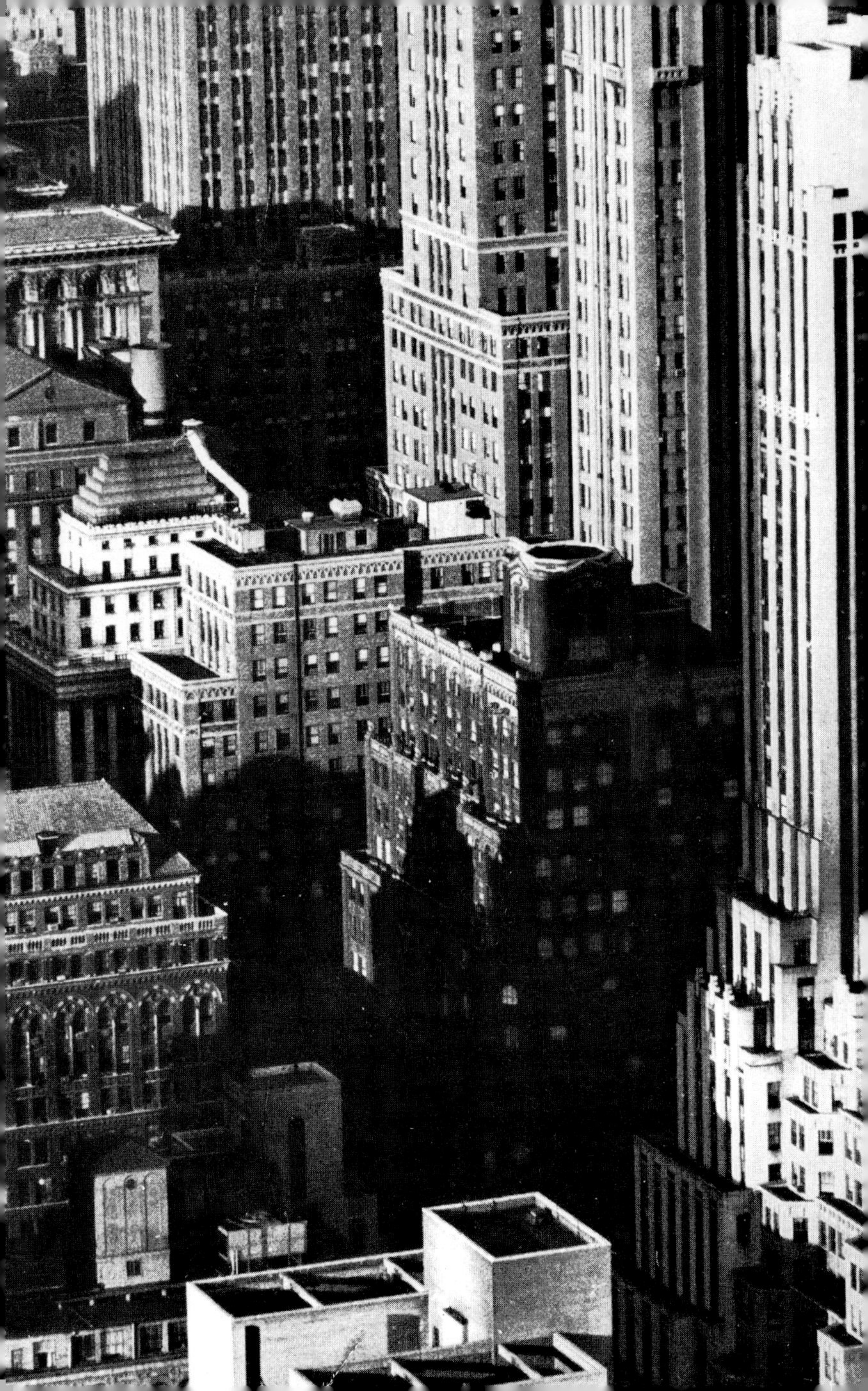

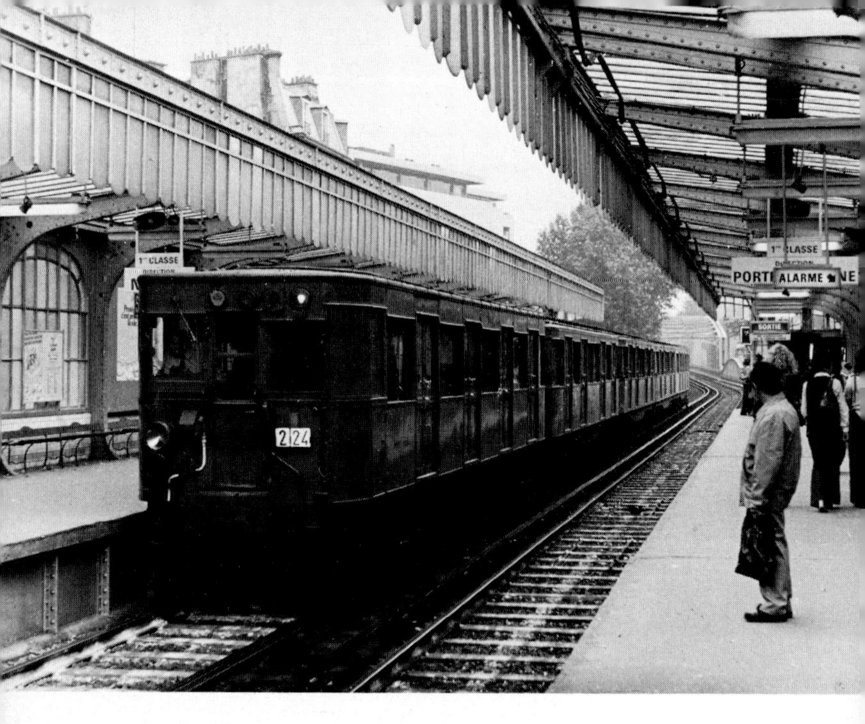

Above.   An ordinary scene, yet it can revive pleasant memories of a holiday. *Clyde Reynolds*

Opposite.   Here the vertical format emphasizes the narrowness of the canals and helps to focus attention on the gondolier. *Beatrice Reynolds*

Previous page.   Some subjects demand an unusual viewpoint, which combined with a change of lens to a short or long focal length can produce a striking result. This picture was taken using a 300 mm lens. *Herbert Keppler*

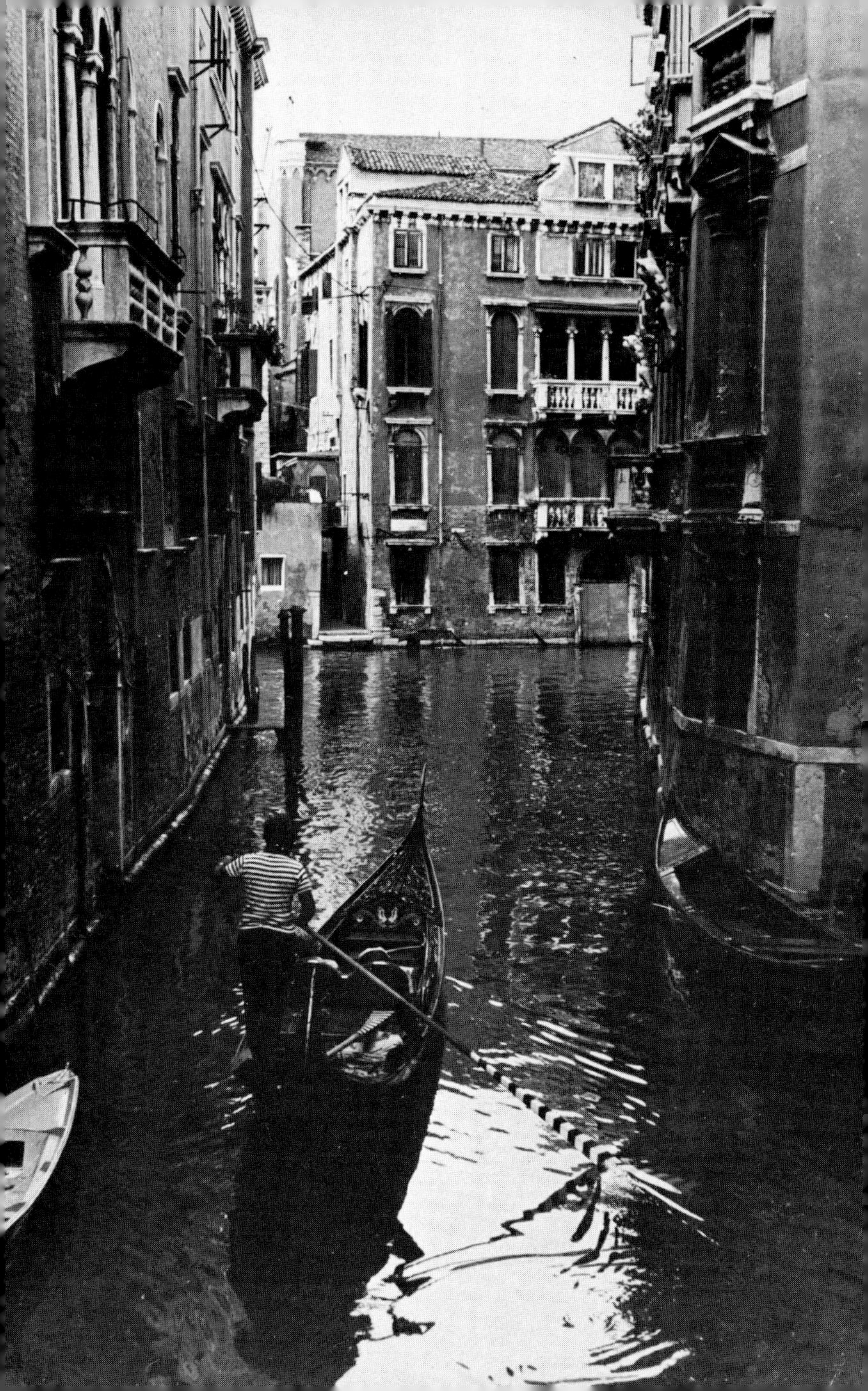

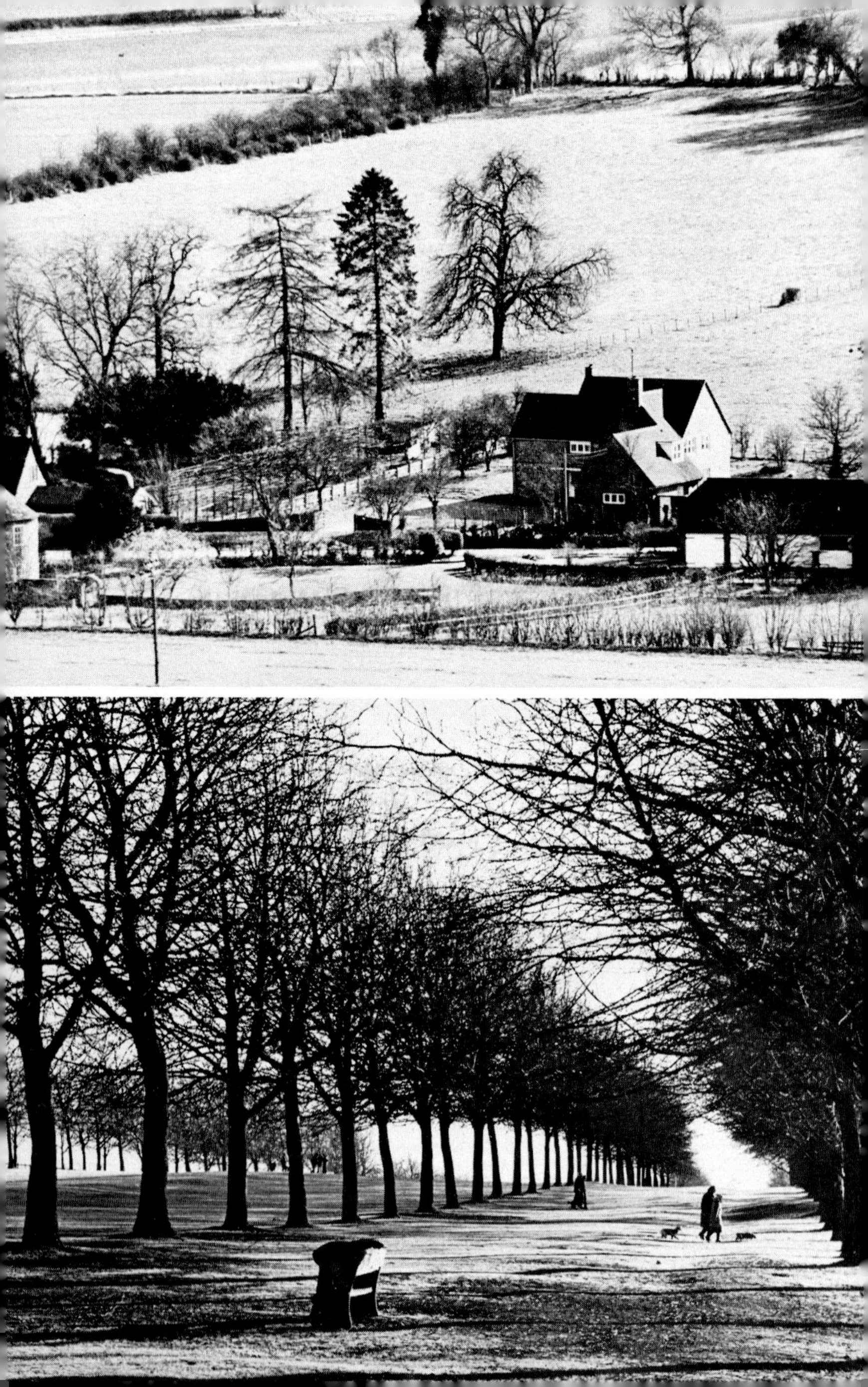

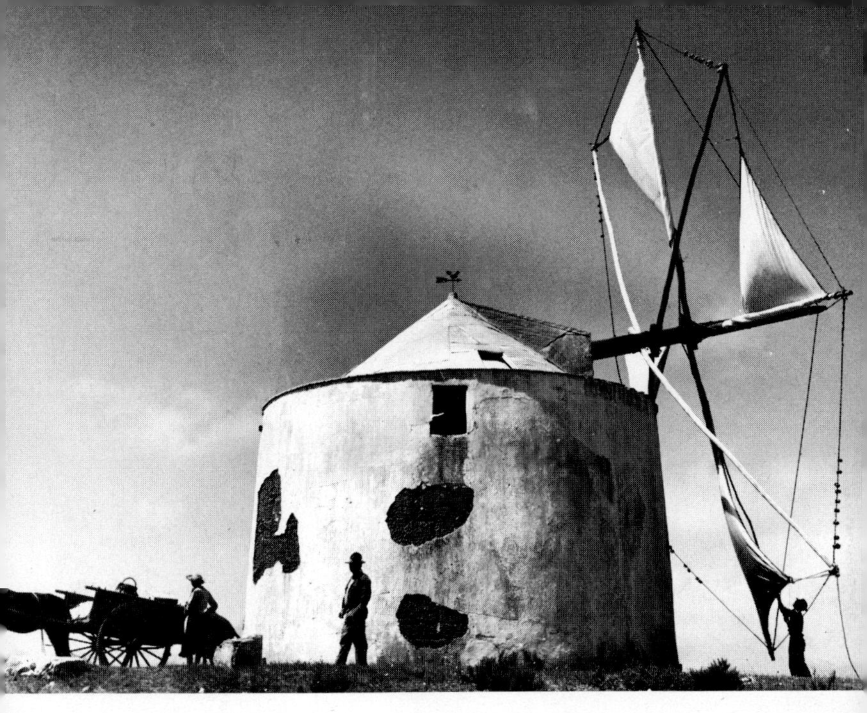

Above.   A low viewpoint removed this subject from a distracting background, making it stand out boldly against the sky. *Arpad Elfer*

Opposite, top.   A long focal length lens tends to compress the various distance planes, zoom lens at 150 mm. *Raymond Lea*

Opposite, bottom.   Converging lines and repetitive design lead the eye naturally along this pleasant tree-lined walk at Windsor. *Raymond Lea*

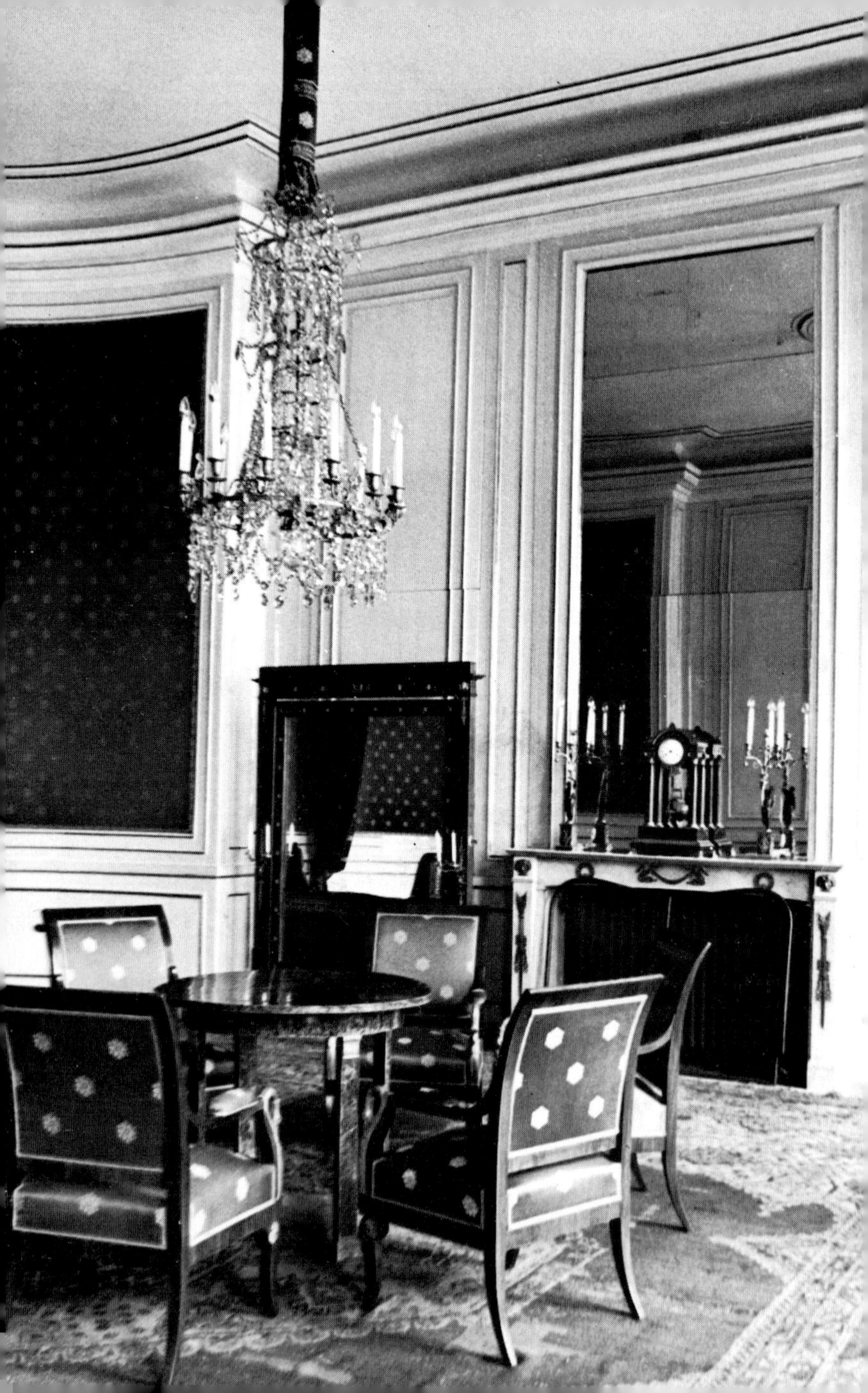

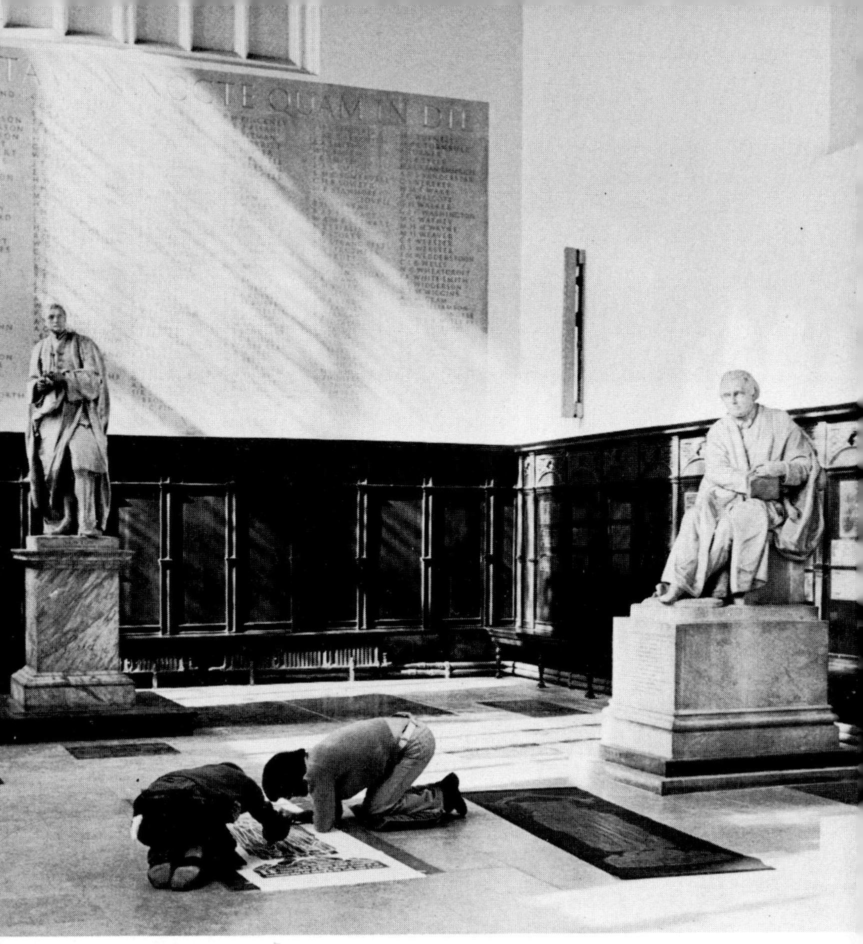

Above.   People in the foreground provide additional interest and give a sense of scale to the surroundings. *Neville Newman*

Opposite.   Interiors often demand slow shutter speeds, large apertures or fast film, or a combination of all three. For speeds below 1/30 sec use a tripod or other firm support to avoid camera shake. *John Rocha*

Overleaf, top.   Autumn mist and weak sunlight provide an attractive pictorial quality to this familiar scene taken with a panoramic camera. *P. C. Poynter*

Overleaf, bottom.   By contrast, bright sunshine gives crisp highlights which stand out boldly from deep shadows to create an almost 3-dimensional effect. *P. C. Poynter*

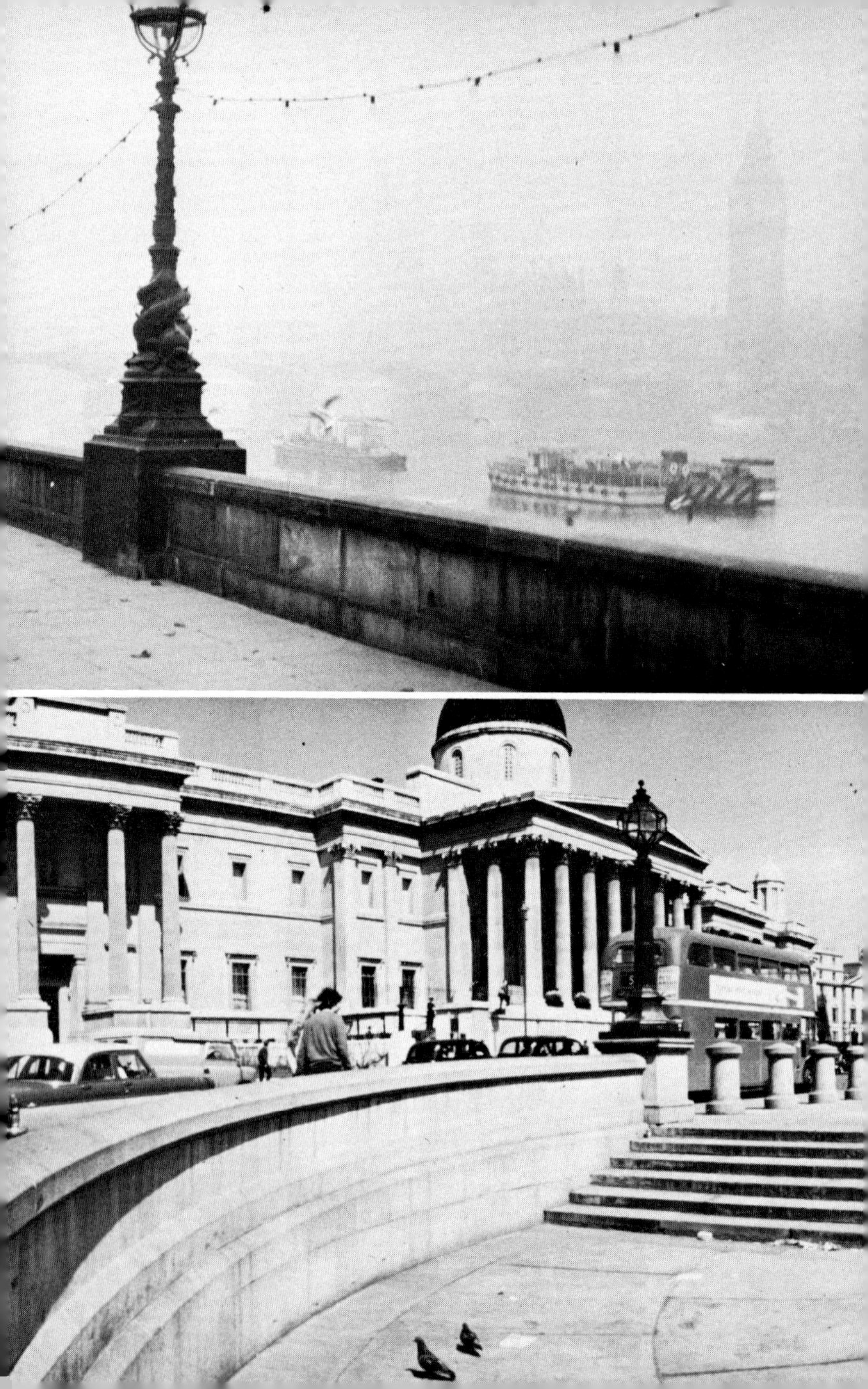

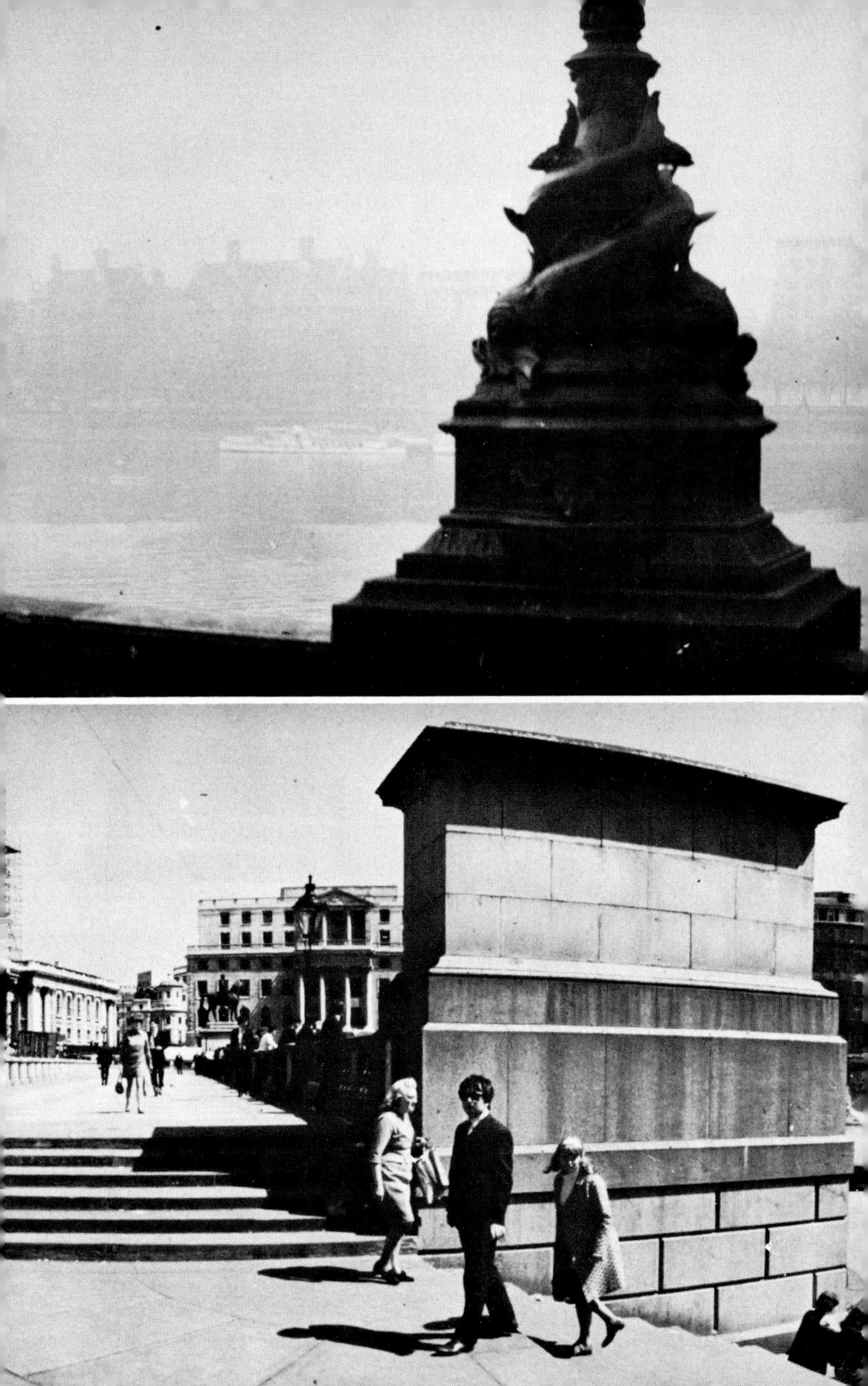

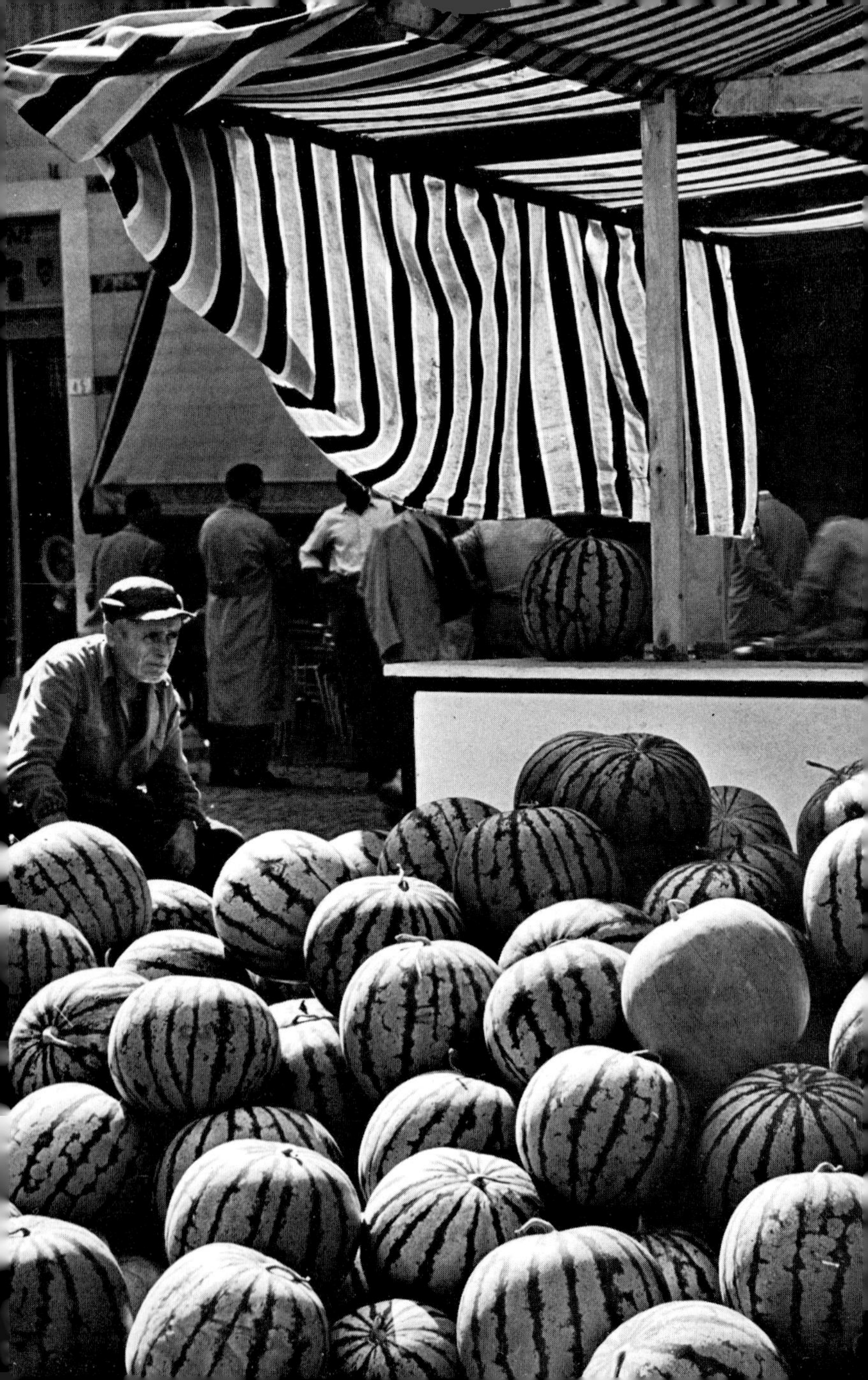

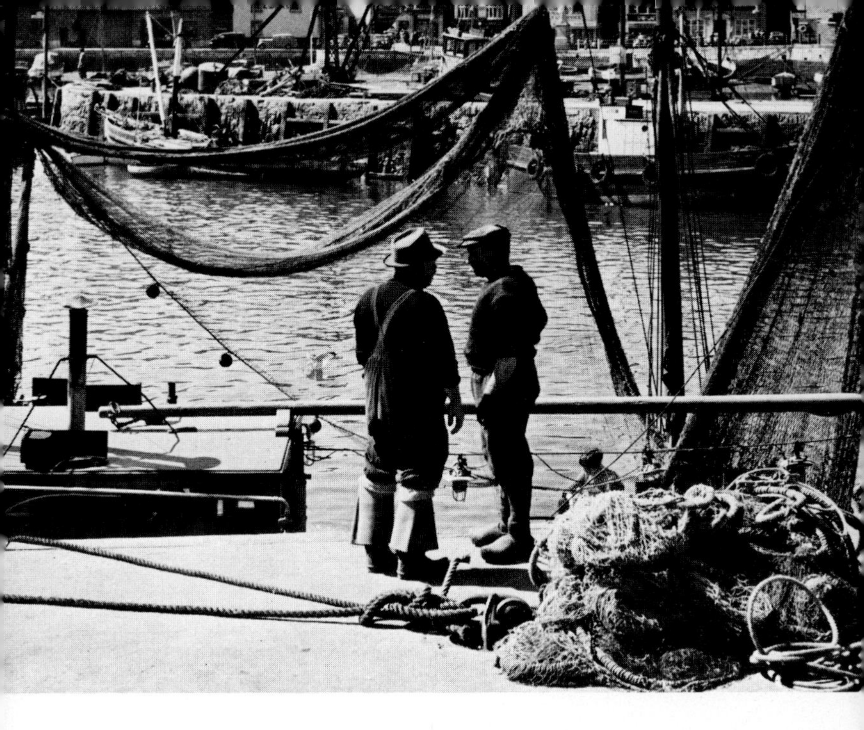

Above.   A familar port scene, but made more interesting by the nets forming a natural frame for the fisherman. *John Blaxland*

Opposite.   Street and market traders are a rich source of pictures both at home and abroad and often typify the character of the country. *J. Le Noane*

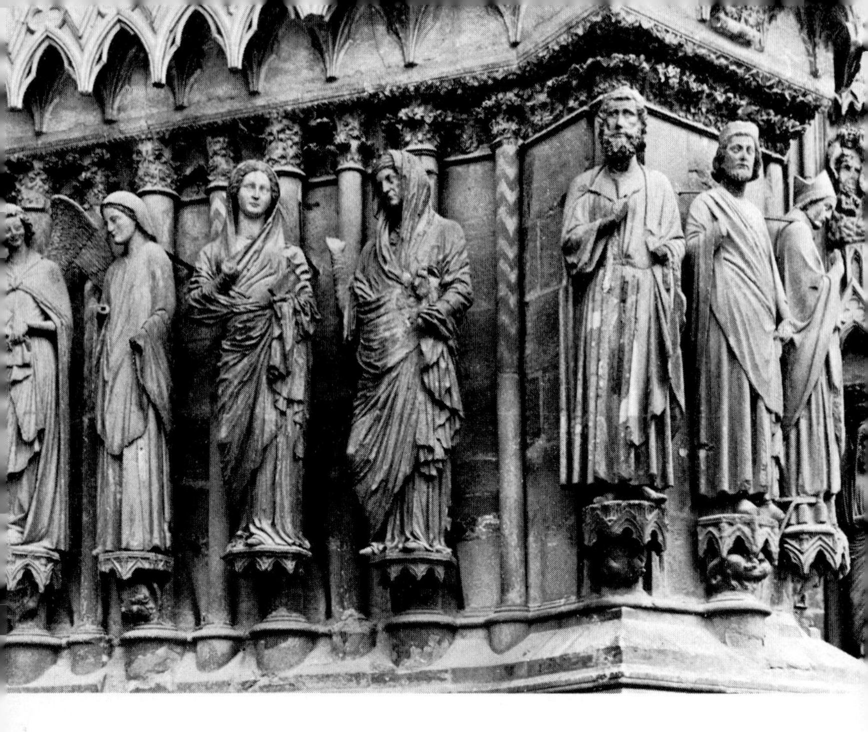

Above.   Architecture usually looks best in bright sunlight, but often shadows obscure interesting details. Here, soft diffused daylight was used to good effect and careful selection of viewpoint prevented the picture from becoming too confused. *Clyde Reynolds*

Opposite.   Strong lighting from above admirably suits the character of this close-up of a carved head. *Neville Newman*

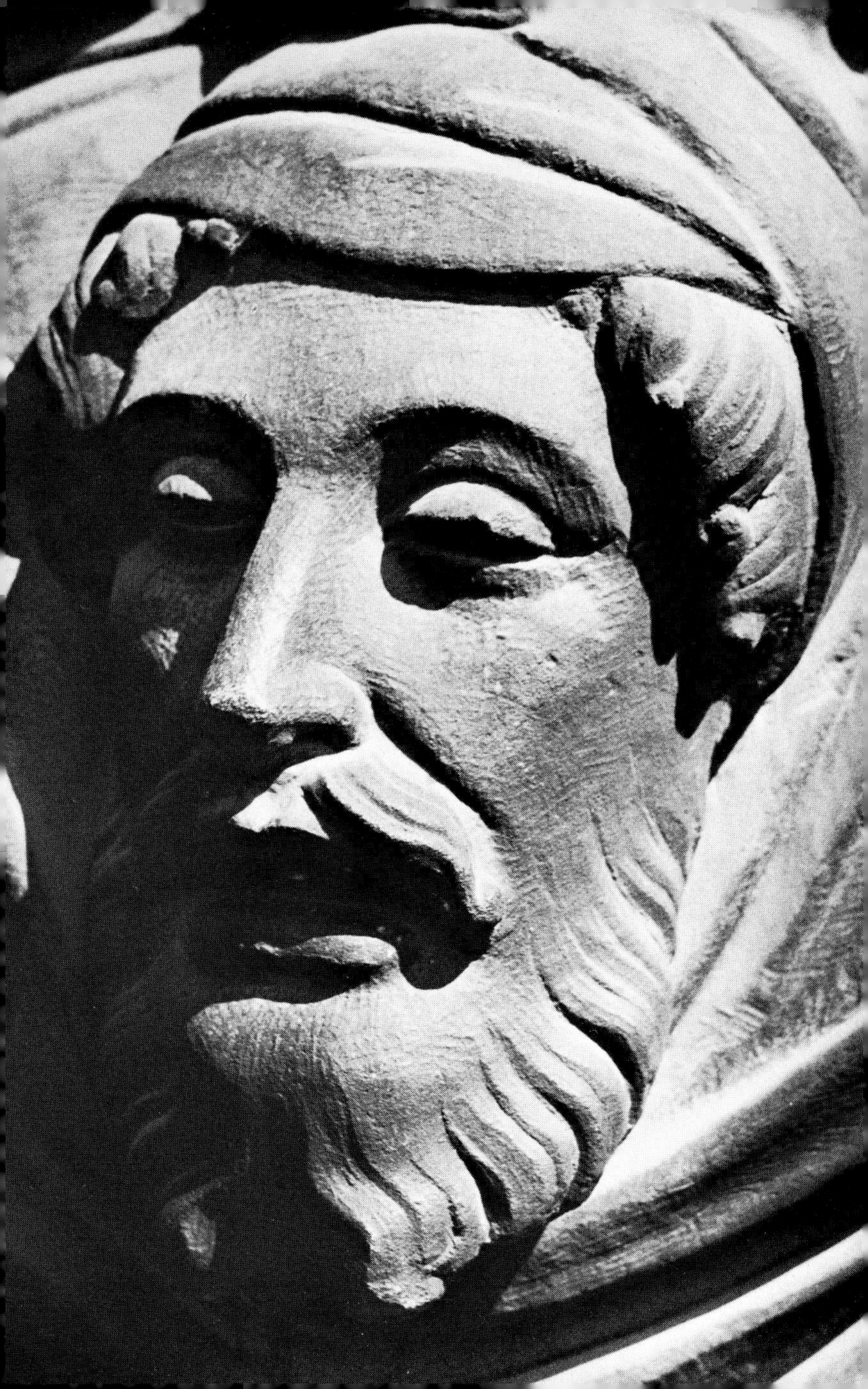

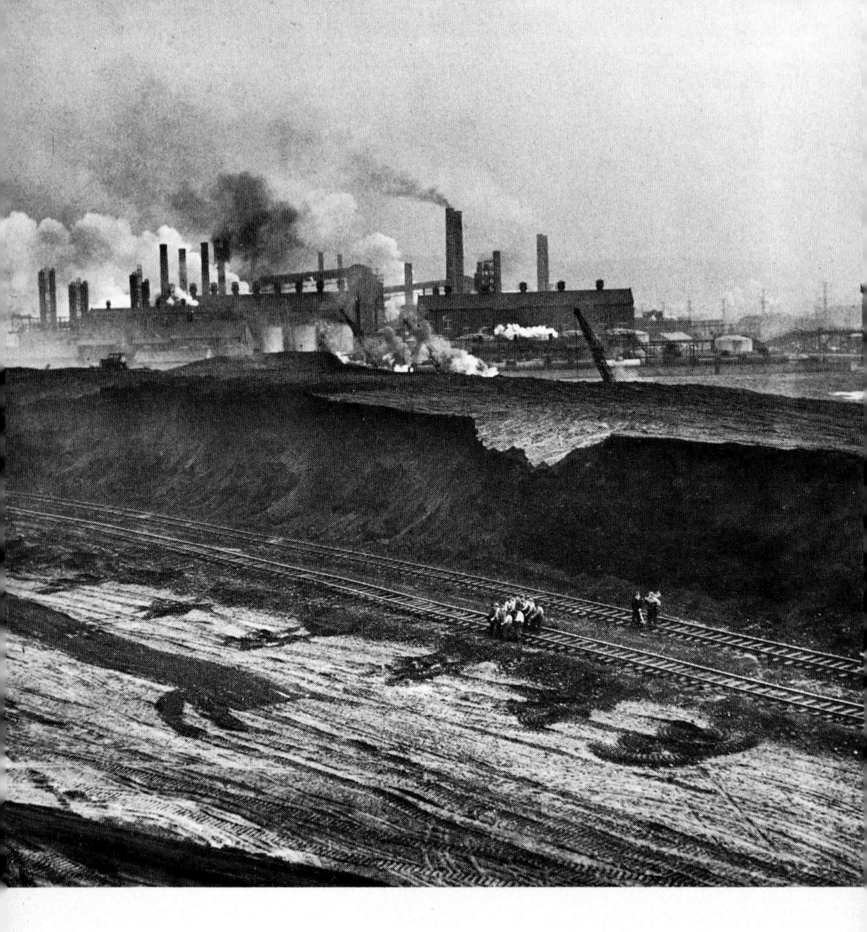

Above.   A high viewpoint turned this unattractive subject on a dull day into a photograph of considerable pictorial merit. *Eliot Elisofon*

Opposite.   It would have been all too easy to shoot this scene 'straight', but a low viewpoint and 'heavy' printing produced a dramatic effect. *Neville Newman*

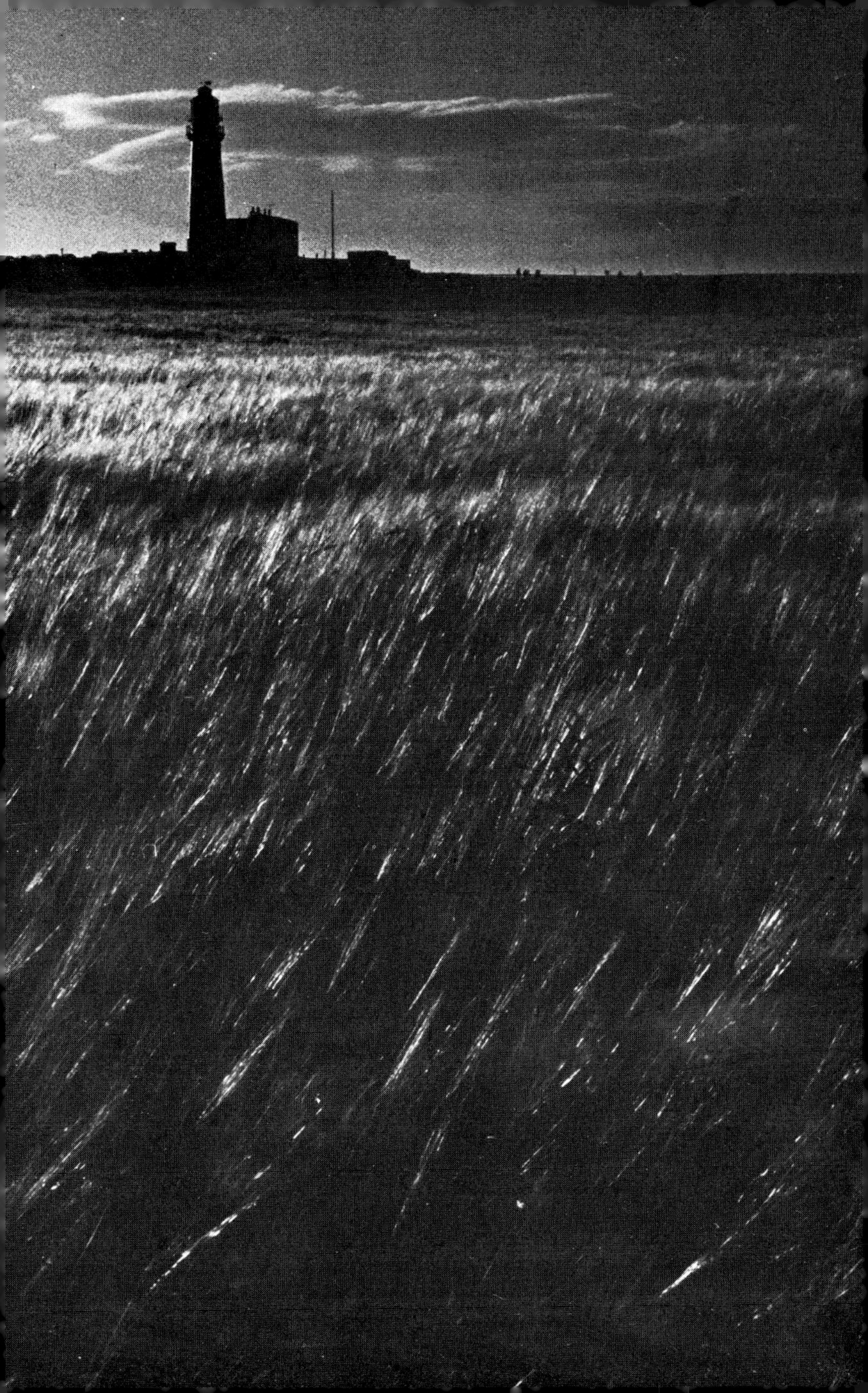

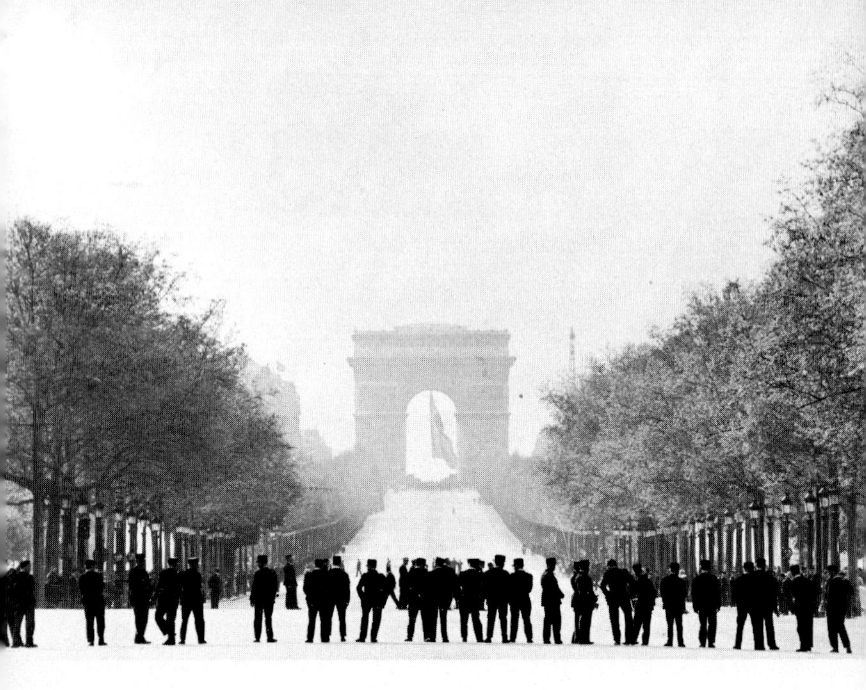

Take advantage of special occasions to shoot unusual views of familiar places.
Piotr Friedrich

pictures. Do not worry too much about movement in the pictures. Most workers remain remarkably still, confining their actions to the job in hand. For example, you should be able to take an adequately sharp picture of a potter, but the pot spinning on the wheel will be blurred. In fact, that blur really improves the picture concentrating your attention immediately on what is happening.

Usually it does need concentration – small workshops are not set up to please the photographer and you will find it extremely difficult to achieve a satisfactory background.

At least indoors your necessarily wide aperture means that most of the background will be somewhat out of focus. Out of door activities often pose the same background problem, but without the saving grace of it being out of focus. However, that does not mean that you should avoid them. No pictorial collection of a marine town is complete without the dockside activity. Such activity can vary from fishermen mending nets to shipwrights cutting up steel plates. Many such shots call for the use of a telephoto lens which allows you to stand well back and out of people's way and out of danger.

Traffic and transport

Mobility is essential to the modern city and while the motor car has become virtually universal, some of its results are an essential part of any townscape. The great highways snaking through the houses, rising on stilts above the smaller ones and swooping through tunnels divide our cities into segments. Their intersections provide dramatic sculptures and even the lines of brightly coloured cars glinting in the evening sun as they shuffle homewards, nose to tail, can form an exciting picture. The classic way to portray them is from above, standing on a bridge and through a long telephoto lens. That way the individual vehicles become crowded resembling a single multi-coloured snake.

The environmentally-concerned point to the great social benefits of using public transport and certainly public transport is of much greater advantage to the photographer, whether on the surface, overhead or even underground. Trains are large and impressive. They and their lines are a striking feature of most modern towns. And the number of people they carry can be equally impressive. We have all seen pictures of station staff cramming people into trains on the Tokyo subway, or of the mass of people clinging to the outside of Bombay's commuter trains, but you do not have to go that far afield to take impressive pictures of the mass of commuters cramming into trains or pouring out of the station. In fact you do not even need the trains, just choose somewhere where the pedestrians are funnelled into a narrow passage – London Bridge is a particularly good example. Every morning thousands flock across the bridge as the commuter trains from the south-east empty their loads south of the river.

When you go to more exotic parts of the world, the means of transport can be ancient, quaint or exotic. Ireland still has a few of its jaunting cars, tricycle taxis and even rickshaws are widespread in parts of the Far East, San Francisco has its cable cars and Bulgaria still some bullock-carts. Unfortunately, these and most other exotic means of transport tend these days to be intermingled with modern traffic, pedestrians and a jumble of roadsigns. To get even satisfactory pictures, you have to go in close, fill the frame with main subject. Sometimes the juxtaposition of ancient and modern can make a nice picture. For example, the intermingled camels and Cadillacs of the oil-rich states of the Middle East.

It is not just pictures of transport which are spoiled by cars. Many old and interesting cities are wrecked by the tin-litter of the rows and rows of parked cars. In the commercial centres they belong to commuters to salesmen and to shoppers or theatre goers, so you may be able to find a quiet day. In Christian countries Sunday mornings are often very quiet, except of course in tourist and entertainment areas. One solution is to go early in the morning – very early – or out of season if that is possible. If you cannot avoid the cars, the least you can do is to minimize their impact on your pictures. Firstly, try and shoot from comparatively high up. Stand on the roof of your car if you are using one. Secondly, choose times when the cars in the particular area that you are photographing are comparatively dull coloured. It is possible to ignore a row of dark-coloured cars where red and yellow ones would be totally unacceptable. Sometimes you can take this a stage further by choosing a time when shadows fall across the cars but not across your main townscape.

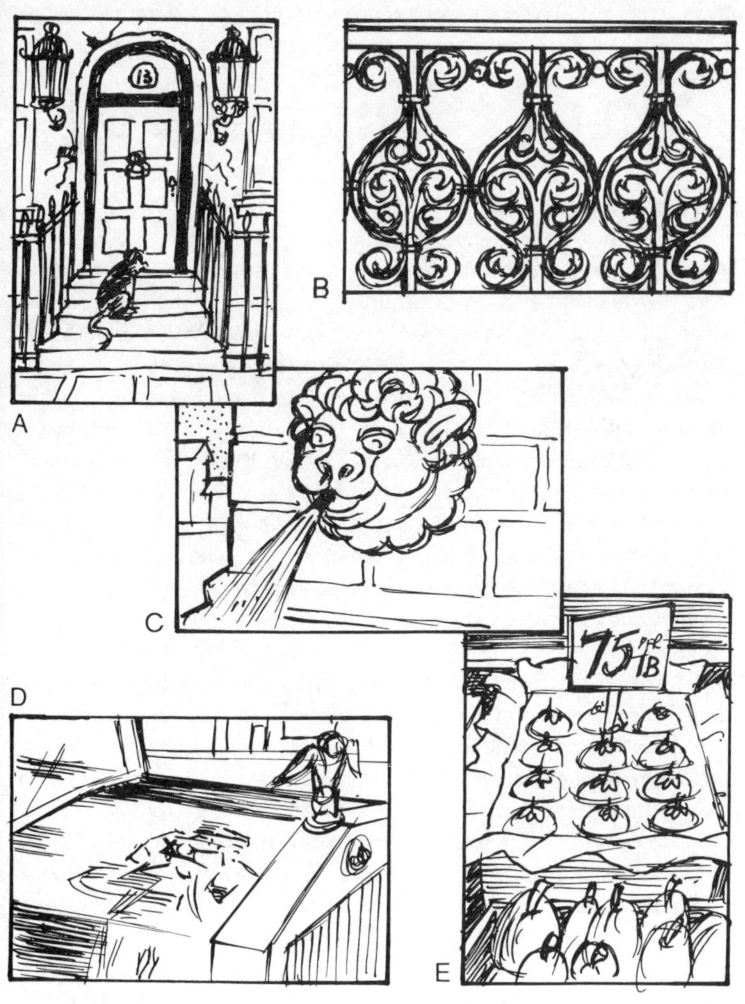

Details can add to your picture story. Often, much local colour comes from the small things in life. A. Doors are an interesting source of pictures, common throughout the world, yet subtly differing. B. The patterns created by builders can be revealing, or just attractive. C. Small detail is worth looking at. D. Reflections and abstractions are another source of pictures. E. Markets and prices tell you a lot later.

If the traffic is constantly moving, you can remove it from your pictures with a long time exposure, in the same way as you can remove people.

People in townscapes

We have talked about people going about their business, and really that is the best way to photograph them. In a market – buying, selling, looking, practising their craft and so on. If you want to include friends, family or a model in your picture, then try to make them look as if they are part of it – not just standing there waiting for you to press the button. Focusing them where you want them to stand, and then get them to walk into shot. If you want them to be doing something, use the same technique and when they reach the appointed place wait for them to start examining the old cameras on the stall or looking at a menu or whatever it is. That way, the whole picture will seem much more natural, at least partly because your subject does not know the exact instant that the picture is going to be taken.

Most people are happy to be photographed; in crowded streets just take your pictures, but if you want to portray a particular person, do ask them first; be especially careful if there is any chance that you will want to publish the picture. Throughout the Western world the law is quite clear that if you use someone's image for commercial gain, they can expect you to compensate them adequately. This is not normally a problem if the people are simply part of a crowd especially in Western Europe. However, close shots of individuals may get you into trouble, especially in the USA. If you go to countries where the people have radically different beliefs, you may find that some or all of the people do not like being photographed. If you suspect that this might be the case, ask somebody who knows first: your travel representative, a colleague who lives in that country or at the hotel to make sure you are not going to get into trouble. In less well developed countries children, and sometimes adults, demand money if you take their picture. It is worth finding out what the going rate is before they ask.

Keeping out of trouble

During World War II my father was photographing a quiet rural scene in Southern England when he was approached by a policeman on a bicycle who said 'You can't photograph there, Sir, it's secret' to which my father answered 'What's secret' to receive the reply 'Can't tell you that, Sir, can I, because it's secret? But if you take a picture of that perfectly innocent-seeming agricultural scene, I'll have to confiscate your camera'. My father never found out what it was that he was supposed not to have been photographing, but it does illustrate the dangers you may fall into. Of course, you should never photograph military installations anywhere in the world, but in politically sensitive countries the list of forbidden subjects is considerably greater. It is unwise to picture soldiers or even police in many parts of the world and even the smallest civil aerodrome is often regarded as being of military importance. The 'Authorities' are often far less polite than a British policeman. The unfortunate conclusion is that if you are unsure of the regime you should confine your townscapes to unashamedly tourist shots, or at least before you get arrested to find out at your hotel or the tourist office just what the local restrictions are.

The sum of the parts

So, to capture a town photographically you need to photograph the buildings, modern as well as historic, its institutions and its transport system, its people going about their daily lives, even the messages sprayed on the walls tell you something about the people who put them there. If you start with a plan you should end up with a logical series of pictures. Perhaps not enough to make comprehensive slide-tape presentation the first time, but certainly something considerably more than a series of totally disconnected snapshots, and together they should be considerably more than the sum of the parts.

Coasts and Beaches, Mountains and Snow

Most of us go to the most interesting places only on vacation. At least, few of us regard the place where we live or the place where we work as being as interesting as the place we go on holiday. There are basically four separate types of popular holiday place: the seashore with its beaches and promise of swimming and boating; the countryside, with its vegetation and wildlife, often of course with some water close at hand; the mountains with their promise of climbing, walking or of winter sport; and towns and villages where the people and their activities are probably the most important part. There is a fifth kind of holiday which actually takes place on or around the means of transport: seaborne – it is a cruise; land-borne – it is a tour. We have looked at the photography of towns, villages and their inhabitants and the countryside, so here we look at the other two major areas; different in many respects, but tied together with their much greater dependence on the weather and by their high proportion of tourism.

Coasts and beaches

The classic holiday beach consists of lots of golden sand, thronging but not too crowded, with happy holidaymakers, the hot sun beating down and the blue sea lapping gently on the shore. It may be idyllic for the sun worshipper, but photographically it can be a disaster. Cameras left in the open sun get extremely hot (if they are not stolen first) which does the film no good; the slightest wind and there is sand blown around. Once that gets inside you are in danger of damaging the delicate mechanism. With the salt-laden air and maybe some spray, you are introducing the possibilities of accelerated corrosion to your valuable equipment.

The next problem is that there is usually rather a lot of light around – often enough to fool a normal reflected light meter and if the sand is at all dark, glaring overhead sun is less than flattering to most people. Light sand reflects up a lot of light, filling the shadows and thus portraits can be quite satisfactory.

As well as being photographically unpleasant, bright sun makes your subjects screw up their eyes unless they are wearing sunglasses – so once again, on the beach, you do not want to be taking pictures with the sun over your shoulder. Turn your subjects round with their backs to the sun – then they can look more natural. There is quite enough light reflected up from the sand and down from the blue sky for you to take a picture even with the simplest camera. If you are using a sophisticated camera, follow an incident light reading or a substitute reading. With a simple camera, set the exposure for cloudy bright.

Simple snapshots

So what are the answers? The first is that if you are going on the beach to sunbathe, swim and play with a beach ball, leave your sophisticated camera behind. It is much safer in the hotel safe. Take a simple 126 or 110 camera with you, and load it with colour negative film. It should take excellent pictures in those conditions and you really do not need to worry about losing it. The important thing to remember, though, is that all the usual aspects of photography – composing the right picture, getting the lighting right, concentrating on your subject and so on – are just as important with a simple camera as they are with any other.

Full-scale photography

When your main aim is to take pictures, of course, then you want all your equipment and you do have to take special steps to protect it. Most of them are commonsense; keep all your accessories in individual polythene bags tightly tied with a rubber band. That way they stay clean and dry even if you drop the bag in the sand, or possibly even the sea.

Take special care of your camera. One way is to cover it with cling film. Set the lens aperture and shutter speed to suit the conditions and use a suitable focus setting for zone focus. With all that light around, you can be quite sure of extensive depth of field. Now you can cover it up with the cling film, leaving the lens poking out through a hole. The film is quite flexible enough to allow you to press the shutter release through it. So (unless you have a power winder, in which case you can cover the camera completely) you need only expose the wind lever to the elements. Of course, in calm weather you do not even have to worry about covering your camera at all — just take special care when you change a lens or load a film. At either of those times, the camera is open and even a slight gust of wind could blow sand into it.

Exposures

Now you have your camera protected, what about taking pictures? We have already mentioned that exposure meters are not necessarily reliable on the beach — the best way to get the right exposure is to take an incident light reading. If you depend on a through-the-lens meter, though, a substitute reading is an excellent alternative. These are all discussed in the Exposure chapter.

Be especially careful if your camera is automatic. Check the exposure that it sets against the substitute reading or even against the information sheet packed with the film. If in doubt use manual exposure or use the exposure compensation dial to give you the setting you want.

The one thing you do not notice, but the film does, is that the amount of UV is much greater by large stretches of water. This can produce a quite unpleasant veil in your pictures, blue on colour film, so you need to use a UV filter the whole time. As always when you use a filter you need a lens hood — sources of flare abound on the beach. Not only is the sun blazing down from above, it is reflected from every wave and often from glasses, bottles and other items used by the holidaymaker.

104

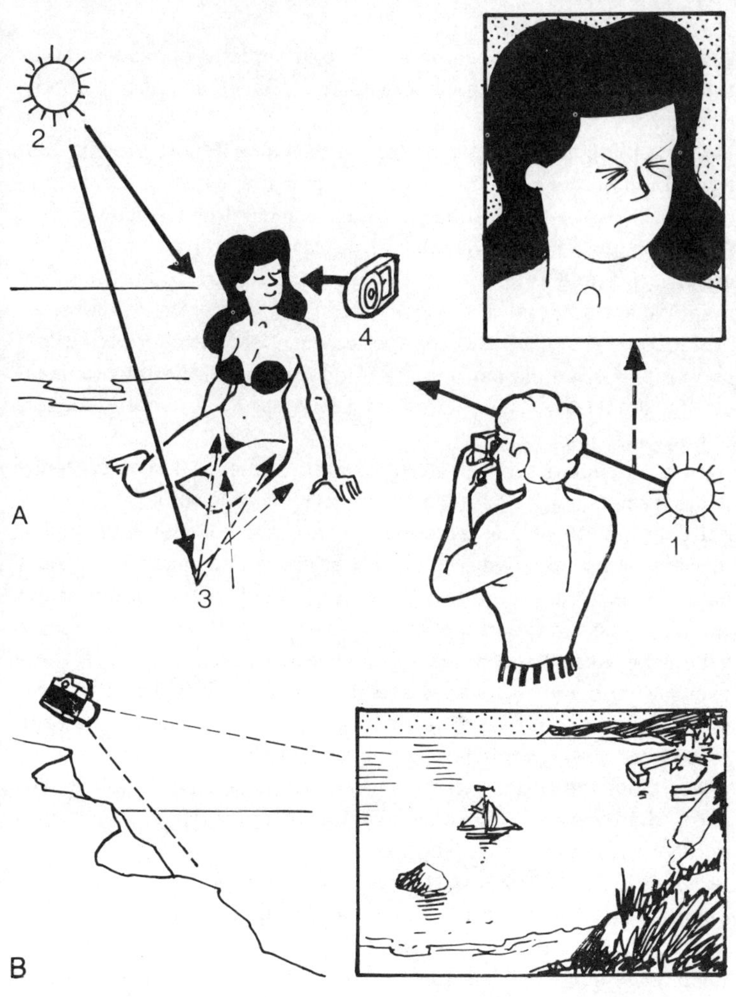

The sunlit beach is ideal for lounging, but less ideal for photographing. A. If you shoot with the sun behind you (1) you are liable to produce squint-eyed portraits. Much better to shoot into the sun (2). The light sand reflects light back to your model (3) and a close-up reading (4) gives you the exposure settings you need. B. From beach level, most seaside resorts are flat and uninteresting. If you can, choose a high viewpoint to produce map-like pictures, which are much more attractive.

Beyond the beach ball

We are here really concerned with photography of places rather than of people, or even holidaymakers. So what special opportunities are there.

The first thing to do is to climb up on the cliffs, if there are any, and look down on the sea. You can often get some almost map-like pictures with the winding coastline stretching into the distance and with perhaps a fishing village or two nestling at the bottom of the cliffs. On a still bright day, the blue-green of the sea makes a magnificient contrast to the beach, even in temperate latitudes.

Tropical waters really are a deeper colour. Near the shore the effect can be one of an almost opaque turquoise and further out to sea a strong almost royal blue. The Red Sea is particularly noted for this strong blue.

Back down again at sea level the water, whatever its colour, tends to be rather insignificant on calm days. In fact your pictures are quite often better if it is rather hazy. Pictures of sailing boats – either moored or under way – look especially good against a hazy background. If there are few boats further out to sea to emphasize the hazinesss, so much the better.

When the weather turns nasty, then the sea becomes much more exciting, with swirling waves and pounding surf it takes on the role of number one subject. The rush and roar and flying of a storm-tossed sea are an impressive sight. Unfortunately, back home in the dry without the sound effects pictures are often disappointing. The spray that appeared to reach the top of the lamp posts appears hardly to wet the promenade rail.

So what are the answers? The first is to thoroughly waterproof your camera. Use it inside a polythene bag fitting tightly round the lens. Make sure the UV filter is tightly screwed on and then go in close. A telephoto shot never approaches the drama of a wide-angle shot which appears to have been taken almost inside the waves. If you are lucky enough to have any sun, shoot directly against it. That will add considerable sparkle to the spray. The choice of shutter speed is very much a personal one. Fine spray is one of the few moving subjects which can be thrilling frozen in mid-air; on the other hand, the swirl imparted by a longer shutter speed can also be an attraction.

While the spray is usually the main subject, do not forget to include some land or part of the boat if you are waterborne – it helps to give some scale. In tropical waters where you have fine coral rock is an ideal ground as it closely resembles, in form but not in colour, spray frozen by a short shutter speed. Wherever you are, do watch the sea carefully for a while before you start taking pictures. That way you can choose a vantage point close to the likely spray points, but not right inside them.

People again!

The coast may well be impressive spread out below you like a map or pounded by high seas. In either case, though, pictures may well give the viewer no clue as to their scale. The best and simplest indicator of size is a person or a group of people. If you are photographing deserted beaches try to arrange for someone to walk across sand – near enough to be more-or-less recognizible – not, though, so close as not to give scale to the main picture. With spray pictures, the choice of position is easy from a photographic point of view – right in it! However, finding people who will happily stand and be soaked with the sea is not so easy. When it is really rough to even attempt to do such a thing could be stupidly dangerous.

Harbours

Near the coast most of the trades are related to the sea; just as with townscapes your coastal pictures need to involve the people who work there. So, a visit to the harbour is a must, not only will that give you pictures of individual activities as we talked about in the last chapter, it will also provide a centre piece to your series of pictures on the whole place.

If it is a fishing harbour you would do well to work out the times the fleet are likely to come in or go out. That depends very much on local conditions. With a deep-water harbour the timing may well depend on the fish market in a nearby big city. Therefore, the fleet may start coming home at 2 or 3 am in the morning so that their catch can be off-loaded and ready for sale in the market by 6 or 7 am. Alternatively, it may be the custom to sell the fish on the quayside, either in the morning or in the evening. Once you have found that out you have one point of reference. In general the time the boats go out is determined by the time they have to come in. It is very often 10 or 12 hours before.

In difficult waters, the boats may depend more heavily on the tides. They may, for example, be unable to get over a sand bar at low water. In that case the times will vary with the tides, as they will if the fishermen want to make full use of the tide. Perhaps they leave the harbour round about high tide so as to go down to the sea as the tide falls, carrying them with it; and then return as the tide rises again.

All at sea

Just as you can take pictures of the sea from the land, so you can take pictures of the land from the sea. The convenience of photography from boats depends on the weather and on the boat. Working from a cruise liner presents no more problems than working on land. On the other hand, working from a 5 m (16 ft) boat in a force 8 gale is virtually impossible.

Between these extremes the difficulties and risks to your equipment increase. Just as with storms and spray on land, if there is a lot of water around keep your camera dry. In fact working from small boats is an excellent reason for having an underwater camera. The metal-bodied Nikonos is a simple-to-use interchangeable-lens camera with a direct optical viewfinder. Assembled properly it remains watertight for all normal skindiving and is particularly suited to rough water marine photography.

In rough conditions, whether or not your camera is waterproof, the danger times come if you want to change a lens or change the film. While you are doing that the camera is open literally to the elements. So it is well worth loading up with a fresh cassette of film before you go; and selecting one lens which is best suited to all your shots. Most often that is a slightly longer than normal focal length; perhaps 85 or 105 mm for a 35 mm camera.

108

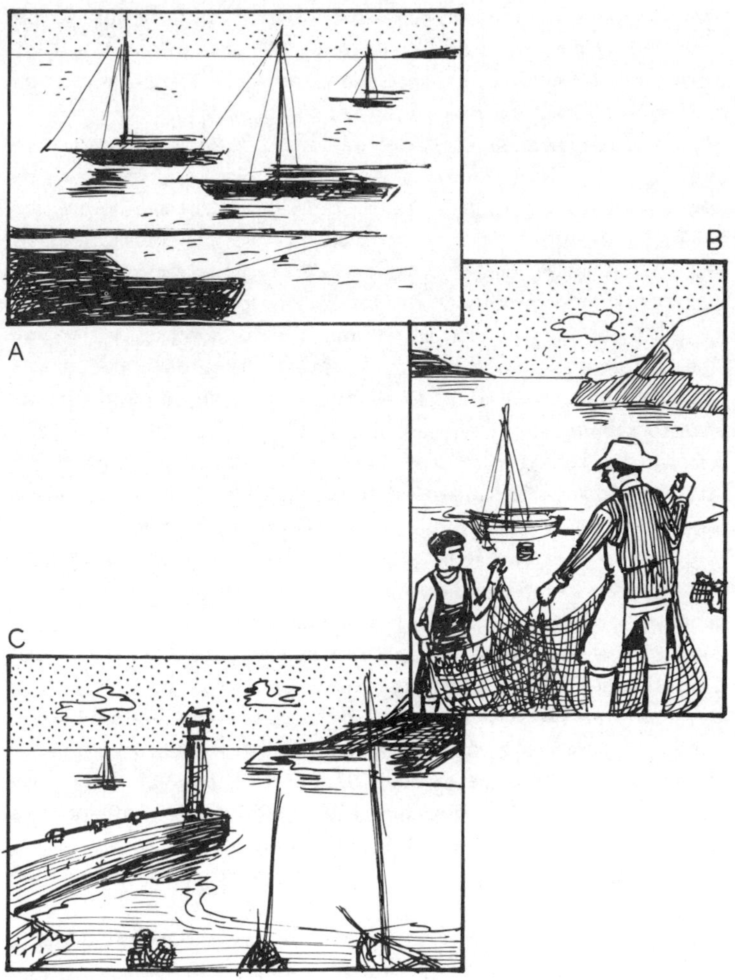

Pictures of places often benefit from man's activity—harbours are particularly photogenic. A. Sea and masts cry out for back lighting. B. People working add much to a series of marine pictures. C. If you walk out along a harbour wall, you can take pictures as if surrounded by the sea.

Such a lens emphasizes the size of the waves on the sea and also enables you to picture the shore with reasonable detail. In moderately calm conditions you might also consider using a zoom lens to give you greater choice. Do not be tempted, though, to use one when it is really rough. You cannot fully waterproof its control collar while retaining the zoom action, and some designs suck in air (and water) when you move the controls.

While a stormy sea can make excellent pictures, most seascapes depend to a large extent on the land you include in them. That can vary from a detailed close-up of the shore, with all its building and activities to an intricate pattern of receding misty shapes formed by rocks and islands. Once you get away from the shore your eyes become attuned to the vast expanse of the sea. Any disturbance of the gently curving horizon stands out in stark contrast. When you look at a photograph, though, what clearly was another ocean liner or palm topped coral atol has become just a minute pimple in the endless boring blue. Once again, you have to examine the viewfinder image with the greatest of care. Ask yourself whether the fact that the blob is the Queen Elizabeth II, Bikini Atol or Tristan da Cunha is actually going to give your picture any significance.

With a real monster lens, of course, you can magnify virtually anything you can see to become a reasonable picture. Unfortunately because you enlarge the effect of any movement with the enlargement of the image, the lenses you can use at sea are somewhat restricted even on the brightest days. Small boats, of course, bob up and down the whole time, while larger ones often vibrate gently to the throb of their engines. With a normal lens, you are well advised to choose a 1/125 or better still a 1/250, second which means you need a 1/250 or a 1/500 second with an 85 or 105 mm lens on a 35 mm camera; and even at 1/1000 second, you cannot be sure of getting pin-sharp pictures with a lens of focal length longer than about 300 mm.

You can often take pictures as if from the sea without setting foot in a boat. Many coastlines are broken up into spurs and inlets; harbour walls curl round so as to virtually enclose a piece of water; and piers are common at least at the more popular resorts and the sea abounds with spurs of sand and groups of rocks. So in many places you can walk out to sea, turn round on your firm dry footing and picture the land. Naturally, if you do that in the middle of a storm you may need some explanation for the spray flying round you.

Shooting against the light

Whenever you picture water or just wet objects, it is well worth while trying to capture the sparkle of the sun's reflections. The classic way to do this is to shoot directly towards a comparatively low sun; with the angle just right every piece of water shimmers and sparkles in front of you. You can include the sun itself in your pictures; but it is usually better if it is just outside the picture area or concealed behind a suitable part of the scene, such as the mast of a ship or the trees on a headland.

The effectiveness of such shots depends to a large extent on their exposure. Surprisingly enough it is well worth starting with a direct reading from the scene. Some of my most effective sun-across-the-water shots were taken on a fully automatic camera with no special compensation. The meter, of course, reacts strongly to the bright points of light and to the sun if you have included that in the picture and gives you a very short exposure, so all the normally lit parts of the scene come out dark, which is the way they look anyway because your eyes give the equivalent of an automatic exposure.

Another starting point is to take an incident light reading and then reduce the exposure by two whole stops. Either way, if the scene is really exciting, then take a whole series of shots changing the exposure at half-stop intervals either side of your starting point.

Bright spots of light in the picture are a real test for your equipment. Lenses with the latest anti-reflection coatings and carefully applied anti-flare interiors, seldom produce strong flare spots. However, the slightest trace of dust or dirt on the lens results in the strong overall veiling with flare. This is certainly one situation where you should not have a filter on your lens just as a matter of routine. Filters are flat — they have to be — and however well they are coated, their flat surfaces are liable to produce flare spots. What is more if you keep a UV filter on your lens to protect it, then by definition that filter is liable to accumulate dirt or to collect tiny scratches because you have to keep cleaning it. Taking the filter off can produce quite a dramatic improvement when you are shooting against the light.

Snow and ice

Photography in winter conditions has much in common with photography by the sea. Conditions tend to be very bright and you can add sparkle by shooting directly into the sun. Once again, you cannot rely on a normal reflected light meter reading; your exposure meter, hand-held or built into the camera, does not know that most of the scene in front of it is pure white snow.

The answer again is to use an incident light reading or to take a substitute reading, from the palm of your hand for example. That really can be effective. I photographed some ski racers in appalling conditions; of course the hillside was covered with snow, but it was also hidden in dense cloud. The skiers appeared out of the white perhaps 30 m (100 ft) away and shot or rolled past. I used the through-the-lens meter to take a reading from my hand and set the camera controls to that. When the film came back from processing I was surprised to discover that the competitors were rather more visible in the transparencies than they had been in real life.

Luckily, most snow pictures are taken in rather more predictable conditions and so you can normally modify a reflected light reading by a standard amount. When the scene consists of little other than snow, two stops extra exposure should be about right. When the snow is a background for people, trees and so forth, then one stop more is about enough. With a fully automatic camera, just set the exposure compensation dial to +2 or +1. If you are not sure which, use the meter to find out. Take a reading from a suitable substitute, such as the palm of your hand, or better still a neutral grey card, and note the exposure. Now point your camera toward the general scene and move the exposure compensation dial until the camera registers the same exposure. While you stay in the same conditions, the automatic exposure system should give you perfectly exposed pictures. In the absence of an exposure compensation dial, with the 35 mm type camera you can instead alter the film speed setting. To give extra exposure set the camera as if you were using a slower

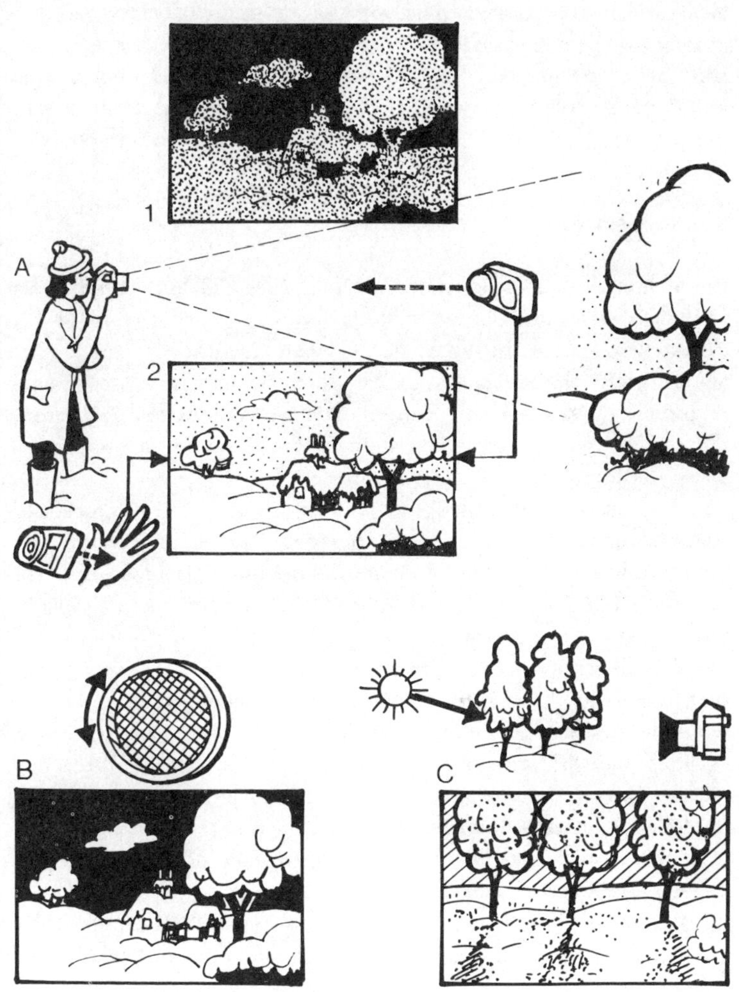

Snow and ice pose their own special problems. A. A direct reading (1) can lead to considerable underexposure, turning the white snow a muddy grey. To achieve the right result (2) take a substitute reading, or measure the incident light. B. The selective darkening from a polarizing filter can often add to snow shots. C. With back lighting, the snow sparkles to add life to the simplest subject.

film. Halve the film speed setting to give you one stop extra exposure or quarter it to give you two stops extra. However, you modify the exposure system, do be sure to put it back to the correct settings as soon as you finish the session. It is much better to think about readjusting it for special conditions each time than it is to have it set incorrectly when you return to normal photography.

Sun and skylight

We all know the snow is white, and unless we look very carefully we see snow as mounds of white stuff; but like any other white object the snow reflects the light that falls on it without changing its colour. Light that reaches directly from the sun is white, maybe tinged with yellow or pink when the sun is low in the sky. Light from the rest of the sky, especially high in the mountains where much snow photography is done, is blue.

You realize just how blue the first time you look at processed transparencies you have taken in the snow. The shadows look quite unnaturally azure. To take more neutral-coloured pictures, you need a suitable filter. The one designed for the purpose is called a skylight filter. It is a very pale salmon UV-absorbing filter and in fact many photographers use such a filter the whole time because it gives them very slightly warmer looking transparencies. In snow, though, while it absorbs UV, thus removing the overall blue veiling, a skylight filter is not really a strong enough colour for many photographers. If you want to reproduce the shadows more nearly a neutral colour then choose a slightly stronger salmon or pale red filter. One which requires an exposure increase of about $\frac{1}{3}$ stop is usually about right.

As virtually all your snow pictures will be taken through at least a UV filter and probably a slightly coloured one, once again you need a good lens hood.

Photography in the cold

Cold conditions affect you and your camera. Whenever you go out to take pictures in the snow make sure that you are dressed to keep warm. Cold fingers make it almost impossible to take sharp pictures. When working in the snow I wear warm clothes with capacious pockets so that I can avoid carrying a gadget bag if possible and soft leather motor-cycle gauntlets. With these gloves on I can take pictures quite easily with a normal 35 mm camera. I need take them off only when re-loading. When photographing sporting events or animals, you often have to wait around for long periods, so footwear is particularly important. Not only should it give you a good grip in slippery conditions, but it should also be warm enough to keep your toes warm.

In arctic conditions, camera problems fall into two categories. The effects of damp and condensation and the effects of the temperature.

When you take a camera out into the cold, the warm moist air inside it tends to condense onto the film and onto the elements of the lens. Although this does no permanent harm, it does make it impossible to take sharp pictures at the time. In extreme conditions, the condensation may even freeze and remain on the camera until you warm it up again. The answer is to let the camera cool down slowly – leave it, perhaps, in a hallway or by a window while you get ready to go out. Then if you have one, put it in a large pocket in your anorak until it is nearly as cold as the outside. Be especially careful of falling snow. If your camera is still warm, the flakes may melt and run in through the camera controls – then as the camera cools, it may freeze solid.

Used with a little care, though, virtually any camera can be mechanically reliable under most normal cold conditions. If you are intending though to take your camera to the Antarctic or on a high-mountain expedition, then consult the manufacturers or their agents about having it lubricated with special low temperature lubricants.

Protecting the mechanical functions is quite straightforward, but dealing with the electronics is a rather more hit and miss affair. The main problem is that mercury cells, and to a lesser extent silver oxide cells which are now more commonly used, can fail to give enough power in extreme cold conditions. When you are selecting equipment the answer is simple – choose a camera which relies on mechanical control for all its normal picture-taking functions and carry with you a separate selenium-cell exposure meter. That way, if the camera's internal meter stops working, all you have to do is use your separate meter and set the controls manually. If you use an electronically controlled camera, you should have no problem with fresh batteries down to about −20° C (about −5° F) and when it is colder still you have to take steps to keep the batteries warm. The simple solution is to keep some spares in an inside pocket; and if the camera appears to be faltering, change them.

Coming in from the cold has its hazards too. Your cold camera, just like your cold spectacles if you wear them, is an immediate target for condensation from the warm air indoors. To protect your camera seal it into a polythene bag before you bring it indoors and allow it to warm up for two or three hours before you open the bag. In fact if you are going out again, and you have no reason to adjust the camera, leave it in the bag until you go out again.

Mountains

Mountains are immense slabs of land but surprisingly often people's photographs make them look like molehills. The reason may be that the shots are taken from too far away, or with too wide an angle lens, but more often it is because there is nothing to which you can directly relate the size. Ideally, you should aim to produce a continuous vista running from recognizable foreground up to the top of the mountain or mountain range. If there is dead ground in the intervening valleys, then you need to give your viewer clues as to how much. Choose a position which shows clearly the relative sizes of similar trees on both sides of the valley, for example. If you are shooting from a long distance with a telephoto lens, the aerial perspective produced by atmospheric haze is likely to give good clues to the distance. More often, though, the standard lens is about right for picturing mountains. With a wide-angle you have to stand so close to the bottom of the mountain that the top may taper into insignificance.

The best place to take a picture of a mountain is from a level of about half way up. While the possession of a helicopter is an obvious advantage for this, the way most people do it is by climbing a

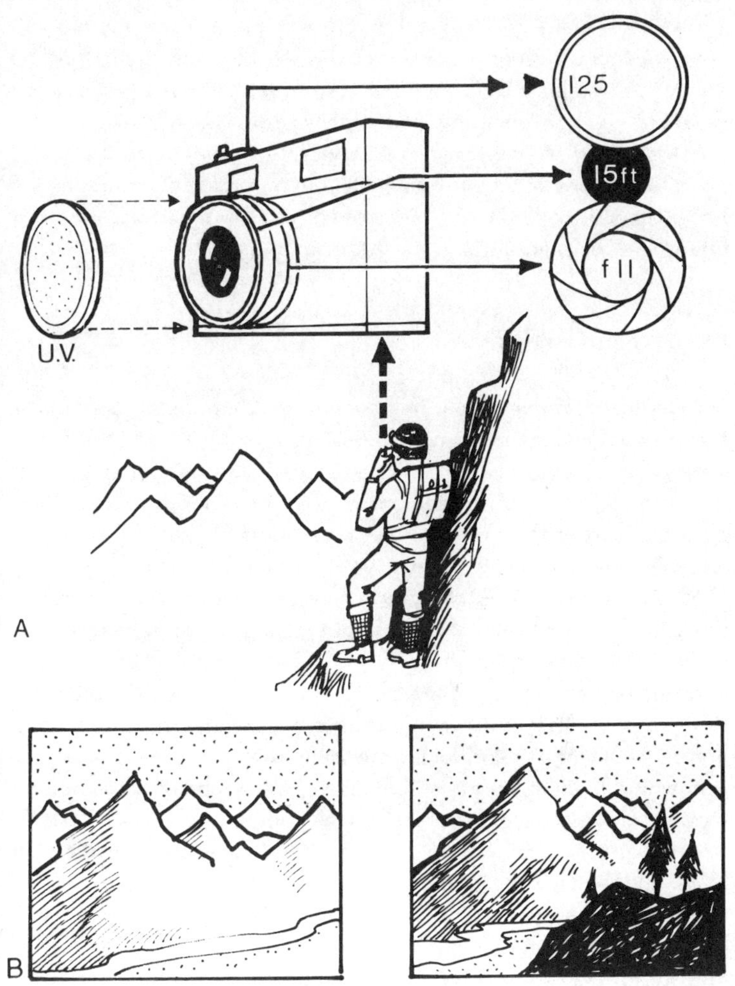

Climbing mountains calls for the simplest photographic equipment. A. A 35 mm 'compact' camera is the first choice. Equip it with a UV absorbing filter, and set it for taking snapshots. All you need to do then is to press the button. B. Mountain shots are particularly enhanced by a suitable foreground.

mountain nearby. When the peak you are scaling is round about the same height as the one you want to photograph, do not go straight to the top – start looking for the right viewpoint when you are half way up. Apart from giving you probably the best viewpoint with the valley below in the foreground, and the hill itself undistorted because you are shooting horizontally. You are also likely to be much closer than you will be when you have climbed to the top.

Just as with any other large subject, your mountain photographs are likely to be considerably improved if you can find suitable foreground or even a frame for the main subject.

Climbing mountains

The dedicated mountaineer has enough problem in getting himself and his companions safely up and down the mountain without being overburdened with photographic equipment. So he probably has a more critical selection of equipment than any other photographer. To a great extent, versatility must take the hind seat; light weight, reliability and convenience must be the major criteria.

This is one field of photography where the rangefinder camera, or the simple direct vision camera reigns supreme. Most pictures are taken at reasonable distances in good light, so sophisticated wide-aperture lenses are quite unnecessary. Precarious positions preclude the use of really long-focus lenses and accessories such as tripods and bulky flashguns are quite impossible to carry.

Perhaps the ideal outfit is a compact rangefinder camera with moderately wide angle standard lens, perhaps between 35 and 45 mm and an 85 or 95 mm medium telephoto. If you work in black-and-white you can do without the telephoto; simply load up with a slow fine grain film and be prepared to enlarge from comparatively small segments of your negatives.

The problems of staying on the mountain and taking your photographs quickly so as to avoid holding up your companions means that you must be able to bring your camera to your eye single-handedly, take a quick shot and put it away. Keep your camera preset on a convenient snapshot setting, say with ultra-slow speed film 125 at f8 with the lens focused on 5 m (15 ft). On more arduous climbs you may even want to tape the controls so that the camera stays at that setting; then you know that every picture will be acceptably focused and properly exposed. Of course, automatic exposure and auto-focus cameras are ideal for mountaineering.

At first sight, pocket 110 cameras seem the obvious choice for most mountaineers. Certainly, with the most recent films their performance is quite adequate. However, while their pocketability is acceptable, very few of them are easily operated with one hand. Their long thin shape makes that extremely difficult. What is more, most of them have facilities only for a wrist strap, and the last thing you want when you are scrambling up mountains is a camera dangling from your wrist. The best way to carry any camera is on a short neck strap, tucked inside your anorak.

The one accessory which makes a camera totally dependent on both hands is an every-ready case, so your camera must go naked. To protect it from knocks, though, and to protect yourself from the sharp corners, you may well be able to use the bottom half of an ever-ready case (with the front top piece removed). The best way to protect the lens is to put a filter on it, and then to use a rubber lens hood to act as a shock absorber. Whatever you do, you must avoid the camera swinging around while you are climbing – not only is it rather bad for it to bang it against rocks, you are also in danger of catching it and the strap on an overhang and getting into a difficult situation.

Pictures after Dark

When the sun goes down, the inhabited parts of the world are lit by man. To our eyes the light appears quite bright because they compensate for its low level. A film, on the other hand, takes a more realistic view. Even with a fast film you have to use a wide aperture lens and a relatively long shutter speed to get acceptable exposures after dark, so you need a camera which can give you at least 1/30 second at f2.8, but that is well within the scope of most sophisticated or moderately sophisticated modern cameras.

Films at night

Most photographers take most of their photographs either by daylight or with electronic flash. These both produce light of around about the same colour and the colour is important when you are taking transparencies. Transparency films record faithfully the colours of the light reflected back to them from your subject and if the light falling on your subject is a different colour, then the picture will be a different colour. In the past, transparency films were produced for a number of different colours of light. Now things are much easier to understand. There are two sorts of transparency film generally available – daylight film or tungsten or artificial light film. Daylight film is the one most of us use, as we have said, most of the time.

If you use a daylight film indoors at night, then you will produce strong orange-coloured pictures; that is because the tungsten lights of most homes is much more orange than daylight. To get natural looking colours with that light you need artificial light film. In fact, artifical light film is balanced for photographic lights which are not quite as orange as domestic lights, but for most purposes it is near enough. If you use artifical light film in daylight not surprisingly you get blue-looking pictures because the film expects the light to be orange and compensates for it.

Instead of using different films you can use conversion filters. In tungsten light you need a strong blue filter, if you have daylight film in your camera. This filter absorbs so much light that you have to treat the fastest films as if they were only moderately fast, and medium-speed films as if they were slow. As tungsten lighting is seldom very bright, this is not a particularly good solution to your problems.

The orange filter which you need to use with artifical light film to take pictures in daylight, on the other hand, absorbs comparatively little light and it is quite practical to keep your camera loaded with artificial light film and use a filter whenever you go out of doors or want to use an electronic flash. However, there is little point in doing that unless you expect to take interior shots.

The colour of most light sources can be quantified as its colour temperature – the higher the colour temperature the bluer the light. Armed with a list of colour temperatures; or, to be even more exact,

APPROXIMATE COLOUR TEMPERATURES OF SOME LIGHT SOURCES

Source	Colour Temperature	Mired Value
Skylight	12000–18000	85–56
Cloudy dull	6250	160
Electronic flash	5500–6500*	182–154
'Photographic' daylight (Daylight film balance)	5500	182
Blue-coated flash bulbs	5500	182
Mean noon sunlight	5400	185
Morning or evening daylight	5000	200
Flashcube or magicube	4950	202
Clear flashbulb	3800–4200	238–263
3400K Photolamps (Type A film balance)	3400	294
Tungsten studio lamps (Type B film balance)	3200	312
Tungsten halogen studio lamps	3200	312
Household lamps 250 watt	3000	333
Household lamps 100 watt	2900	345
Household lamps 40 watt	2650	377

*Most small modern units have a tinted discharge tube to bring them close to 5500K and sometimes lower.

a colour temperature meter you can select exactly the right filter to make subtle changes to the colour of your pictures – this is all described in detail in the *Focalguide to Filters.* Here we will just reiterate that when you take transparencies by tungsten light you need artificial light type film to give you a neutral colour balance.

Long exposures

Some night pictures call for extra-long exposures; and films can react oddly to them. At exposure times longer than 1 second or so, films become less sensitive. So, for example, if your meter suggests 8 second at *f*11, you actually may need 8 second at *f*8, or 16 second at *f*11.

The actual change (called Reciprocity Law Failure) varies from film to film. If you intend to make a lot of long exposures, it is as well to get the information from the film manufacturers. Otherwise, just bracket your exposures by 1 and 2 stops more than the meter suggests (i.e. take 3 in all).

Unfortunately, colour films may produce unusual colours as well. That is why each film is given a recommended exposure range. However, few night pictures of places depend too much on accurate colour, so this should not worry you.

Street lighting

Our roads are illuminated by a whole variety of lighting varying from brilliant tungsten halogen units high overhead, like those in Edinburgh's Royal Mile, to the occasional Victorian gas standard left over from a previous era. Most modern street lighting uses gas discharge or fluorescent tubes. This is very unfortunate for the photographer. The yellow orange of sodium vapour lamps records on most colour films a strong red, even with modern high pressure varieties which are much better to see by. The older type of green-purple mercury vapour lamps come out an even more ghastly colour – a lurid green; and most fluorescent tubes also give a pale greenish light in photographs. So where street lighting is the only source of illumination you are virtually confined to black-and-white work.

In commercial areas, there is a far greater range of light source. Shops, restaurants, theatres and so forth pour out light from their windows; and buildings are often covered in towering hoardings glowing with light of all colours. In brightly lit shopping areas anywhere in the world, you can take hand-held pictures with 400 ASA film. Base your exposure either on an incident light reading or on a selective reading from, for example, your subject's face. It is usually around 1/60 sec and at $f2.8$ or $f4$. That is quite adequate to show people doing things, but with most lenses the depth of field is still limited and you are certainly not going to get a sharp picture from here to infinity.

Picturing lights

When you take pictures of the lights themselves it is a different story. Again with 400 ASA film, even a modest local advertising display is probably bright enough to allow you to use 1/60 second at $f5.6$ or $f8$. Really brilliant displays, such as London's Piccadilly Circus or Las Vegas' Golden Mile, let you close down possibly to $f11$ and still use 1/60 second. That allows you to take sharp pictures of signs a considerable distance apart. Many advertising signs flash, but few of them move, so if you can keep your camera completely steady on a tripod or resting against a solid object, you can safely use much longer shutter speeds and so use small apertures with quite modest displays.

Sometimes the displays themselves are enough to make a photograph. More often you need something in the foreground; brightly lit shop windows and the blur of passing traffic are often successful but can get rather monotonous. Undoubtedly the most exciting foregrounds are those which reflect the light, so despite the discomfort it is often better to take your night shots in the rain, so that the pavements glisten with myriad reflections. Of course, where you can find a river, fountains or perhaps a lake, then you need not wait for the rain.

It is not just advertising signs that provide interesting light pictures – many holiday resorts are decorated with coloured lights for the season and so are the centres of many towns for festivals such as Christmas. A record of illuminations such as these is obviously an important part of your portrait of any place.

Floodlit buildings

When people are proud of their buildings, they shine bright lights at them at night. The effect is particularly impressive from a distance and always an invitation to the photographer. They are a subject which is particularly appealing in black-and-white. One reason for this is that most buildings are floodlit from ground level and in fact the light falls off quite considerably toward the top of the building, so the top is quite often lost in the dark. On a colour transparency, there is little you can do about it. On a print you can correct to some extent, and the fall-off is usually less noticeable in black-and-white than it is in colour.

On the other hand, buildings lit from inside almost always benefit from colour even though the fluorescent tubes in an office block may vary in colour from window to window. Given a reasonably long exposure, that just adds interest to the picture.

In a colour shot, whether the building is lit from inside or from outside, you often want to include a deep blue sky as well. Theoretically, there is a point each evening when the light from the sky balances the artificial light on the building. In practice, that is difficult to determine. If you can, it is much better to make your picture with two separate exposures.

In the early evening, mount your camera on a tripod and line it up with the building; take a meter reading from the sky and give about three stops *less* exposure than that suggests. Re-set the shutter on your camera without winding on the film. If it has a multiple exposure system that is easy; otherwise it may be more of a fiddle and with a cartridge-loading camera it is quite impossible. Do not disturb the camera at all; just wait until the lights on the building are illuminated. Then take a normal, fully exposed picture of the building.

Moving lights

Now we have introduced a tripod and, of course, a cable release which you need to take steady pictures, we can look at some more possibilities for using a static camera at night. Most night scenes consist of a series of points or possibly bars of light against, what is to the film at least, a totally dark background. If these blobs move while the camera shutter is open, they become streaks in the picture, which gives you another way to picture places.

Fun fairs, such as the enormous one which accompanies Munich's October Festival and provides entertaining interludes between the more serious sessions of drinking beer, become at night seas of moving lights. Point your static camera toward any of the bigger entertainments – a ferris wheel, the big dipper, the octopus, or a roundabout and hold the shutter open for a few seconds. Your pictures will be a fantasy of dancing lights.

The next most popular subject for this sort of treatment is a traffic interchange. Approaching cars describe lines of white, or in France yellow, light with their headlights; and retreating ones dimmer but usually still visible red streaks. Direction indicators add their own individual effect to photographs. They produce a line of dashes – white amber or red as you might expect; and the effect of sequential flashers can be even more entertaining.

As it is the lights which are forming the picture, exposure is not too important. With a medium-speed film, try an aperture of around $f11$; with a fast film of around $f22$. Decide on the length of your exposure by the amount of movement you want to get into the picture. Remember that, for example, with motor cars the trail left by one blends into the trail left by the next, and times of around half a minute are very often ideal.

Lightning

Storms during the day can make spectacular pictures; those at night even more so. To picture lighting again you need your camera on a tripod, face it towards the storm. You can soon see where the majority of flashes are. Set the lens to infinity and stop it down to about $f8$ or $f11$, then open the shutter. Close it again after a single flash or when you feel you have seen enough flashes. Usually objects on the skyline appear as silhouettes, but after a number of flashes or if the moon is out you may get some detail in them, which can very much improve the picture.

One of the best thunderstorm pictures I have seen was taken across Lake Tanganyika some years ago. It was produced by a half hour exposure and showed half a dozen or more forks of lighting apparently striking the hills on the far side of the lake. Each flash had illuminated a different part of the sky so as to give an impression of the storm clouds from which they were coming. The lake in the middle distance was covered with lines of light produced by the lanterns on the little fishing boats dashing for shelter before the storm reached the water.

Moonlight

The light reflected from the moon is a very pale imitation of that directly from the sun. With very long exposures you can take perfectly good pictures by moonlight. However, if you really do give enough exposure for the film, the result is just a rather odd and apparently daylit picture. This can work in colour, but usually the colour is distorted because daylight-type films are not designed to be exposed for half a minute or more.

It is perhaps more intriguing to take pictures which look as if they were taken by moonlight – think for a minute what your impression of a moonlit scene is like – most people imagine it as dim and rather blue. In fact, the light is usually so dull that our eyes cannot distinguish colours at all.

To take a dim blue scene, you need to put a blue filter on your camera and give rather less than the normal exposure. The filter most commonly chosen is the one which you need if you are going to expose daylight film to tungsten room lighting. This filter demands that you increase the exposure by nearly 3 stops to get a normally exposed picture. For a moonlit effect, you probably only need to open up by 1 stop from the metered exposure for your film without the filter on it. Of course, a through-the-lens meter measures through the filter as well, and so if you have an automatic exposure camera, you must use the exposure compensation system to produce the underexposure you want. Instead of using a filter you can take the pictures on tungsten light film in daylight and underexposed – that has the same effect.

Indoors at night

We discussed just a little about the problems of photographing buildings inside by daylight. At first sight, once the lights are on, things would appear to be much easier, but that is not always the case. Lights in the home are placed so that people can see what they are doing. In museums and galleries they are placed to illuminate the displays. Even when the building itself is the subject on display, the lighting is normally arranged just to pick out details. What all this lighting has in common is that it is extremely uneven. Patches of light where they are needed – dark corners, nooks and crannies elsewhere. While that is quite acceptable to someone standing in the room, it can look very odd in a photograph. However, if you are aware of the problem you can usually work round it. Confine your shots to details, perhaps, or sections of a room where it is quite obvious why the light is patchy.
Despite the patchiness, you usually get the best results with a transparency film by basing your exposures on a meter reading from the light reflected from the brightly lit areas. Of course, if they are unusually light or dark, you must either modify your exposure settings or use a substitute reading. One point to bear in mind: most built-in exposure meters are rather oversensitive to red light, so they tend to overestimate the light level indoors. If in doubt, give $\frac{1}{2}$ stop more exposure than the meter indicates. With an automatic camera, use the exposure compensation dial or adjust the film speed setting.

What about the colour?

As you have seen from the table, no film is balanced exactly for the normal sort of tungsten lighting used indoors. With colour negative film, as we noticed, it really does not make any difference, and in practice a tungsten-type transparency film gives quite acceptable results. Remember that if you underexpose a transparency film, the colours become more saturated and vice versa; so when the lighting balance is not quite right, if anything err on the generous side. That will tend to make the differences less obvious.

Sports

No series of photographs on a place can be complete without representative pictures of its indoor sports. Most sports take place sometimes indoors, or outdoors after dark. These events are lit by batteries of floodlights from above. Usually the playing surface is quite a light colour and reflects back enough light for you to take reasonable photographs. At important events, the lighting is really quite bright – it has to be to allow colour television cameras to work. Bright lighting is particularly useful at sporting events, because they combine two of the photographers greatest problems: things happening at distance, and movement. Even the professionals, with their press passes to photograph the event, will be using very long-focus lenses at times; and anyone working from the terraces is going to need at least 180 mm on a 35 mm camera. Really wide aperture telephoto lenses are becoming available, but are beyond the reach of most enthusiasts. So, you are likely to be working with the fastest films at around 1/60 second at $f2.8$ or $f3.5$. At that shutter speed through a long telephoto lens, you cannot hope to freeze action.

That leaves you two ways to treat the subject. Either select stationary points or pan with the motion so as to deliberately blur the background. In fact some of the most effective pictures are events like gymnastics, for which the photographer has chosen an extremely long shutter speed so as to show an action or a whole sequence of actions as a continuous blur. This is a technique particularly suited to indoor meetings because the competitors are brightly lit and often standing out against the dimly lit background of the audience.

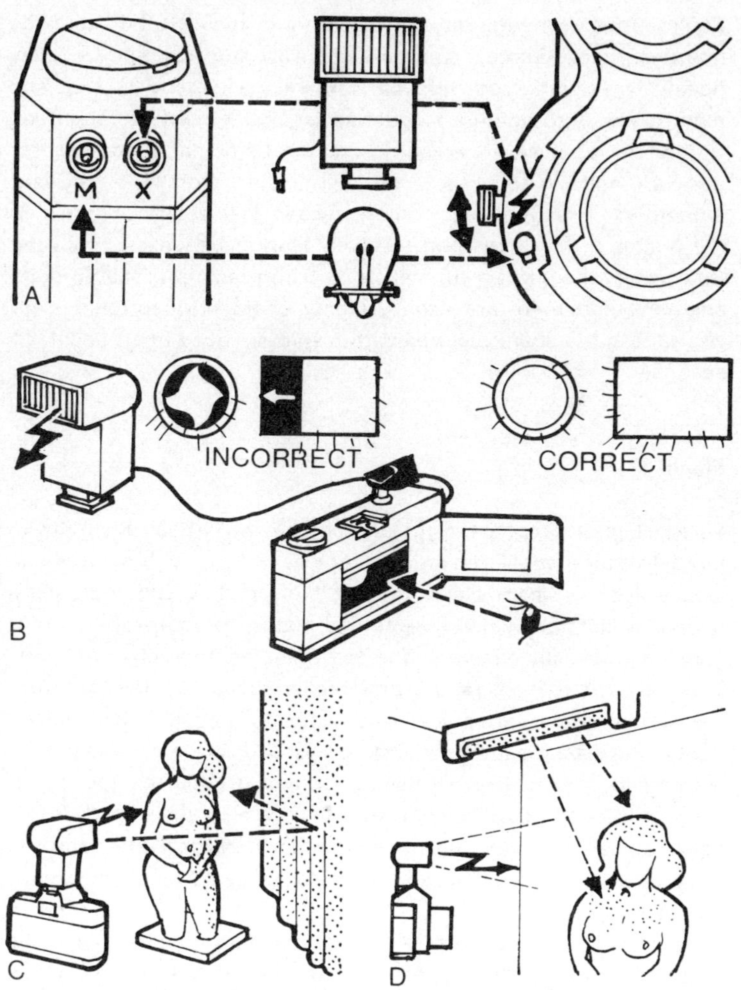

Flash is useful for nearby subjects after dark and indoors. A. Make sure that your flash is connected correctly. B. You can see quite easily with an electronic flash by looking through the back. C. Even in flash pictures, beware of false colours, from a bright coloured reflector. D. The ambient lighting can colour your flash shots, especially if you use a small flash.

Entertainments

Public entertainments vary considerably in their attitude towards photographers. Some, such as circuses and ice shows, may positively welcome you with your camera, while many theatres and night clubs try to enforce a rigid ban on photography. If you intend to photograph such an event, do find out beforehand whether it is allowed and if necessary ask permission from the relevant authorities. Assuming you can go ahead you are once again in the realms of fast films and relatively long-focus lenses. From the front rows, though, an 85 mm or 105 mm lens is probably quite adequate and there are usually plenty of static opportunities for you to take pin sharp pictures with a shutter speed of around 1/60 second.

Flash

To most photographers night photography calls flash instantly to mind. With the small and convenient electronic units now available simple flash is there for everyone. It is great for photographing people or animals, small insects and plants, for close-ups and for copying; but really has very little use in the photography of places. There are two reasons for this both related to fact that the light from a flash diminishes very quickly with subject distance. In fact, as you double the distance from the flash to your subject, so you reduce the lighting to one quarter. Really someone must tell the tourists at Niagara Falls one day. They happily go flashing away with their tiny light sources, hundreds of metres (yards) from the water, and like most other places the falls are far too far away for the flash to have any effect at all.

That is the first reason: places are just too big for most flashes. The second reason is that pictures of places, at least those taken following the advice in this book, have a foreground, a middle ground and a background. If your flash is powerful enough to illuminate the middle, then your foreground will be burnt out by being overlit and your background still unlit. So keep your flashgun to take pictures of people doing things.

Painting with light

There is one rather complicated technique which you can try with a flash or in fact with any other portable light source if you have, say, the interior of a large building to yourself to photograph; it is called painting with light.

The way you do it is to set up your camera on a tripod focused on the darkened interior; set the shutter to 'B' open it and lock your cable release. Now walk round the building pointing your flash to each sector in turn and firing it with its open flash button. With careful planning and execution you can take a very good photograph like this.

Remember that as with any other flash pictures, the lens aperture you need is determined by the flash to subject distance; so, for example, you may choose an aperture which requires a flash to subject distance of 3 m (10 ft). Then make sure that each time you fire your flash it is about $4\frac{1}{2}$ m (15 ft) from the nearest subject. To get an even coverage of light you will have to overlap the flashes very considerably so this should give you about the right exposure level. As you build up the picture, work to a plan which gives you some gradation in lights to provide the modelling you require to reveal the shape of the room. Remember, too, to stand well to one side as you fire the flash otherwise your silhouette will appear many times in your picture.

What Sort of Equipment

You can photograph places with any sort of lighttight camera, including one made from a cardboard box! Owning a simple camera will not stop you taking good pictures, and owning an expensive one will certainly not guarantee that you will. All an expensive camera does is to give you more control – if your camera has variable aperture setting and a range of shutter speeds, then you can shoot in poor lighting, include fast-moving subjects in your pictures and control how much of the picture will be in focus. A wide-angle lens lets you get in closer and still include all the picture; a long-focus (telephoto) lens lets you get further away and so on.

However sophisticated it is, a camera cannot find pictures for you; but the more versatile your equipment, the more pictures you can make. Only you can make those pictures, though.

Simple cameras

I have a whole collection of simple cameras – 126 cartridge-loading ones. Sometimes I want to take a picture purely as a record. I can do that reliably and easily with my simple camera. If I am taking pictures when the camera might get damaged, for example, if I am at sea with the waves breaking over me, then a simple camera is less costly to replace – and the pictures it takes are good enough for what I want.

Sometimes, too, I take a simple camera out to make pictures. Even if you have a more expensive camera, I recommend this as an exercise. You cannot stand where you want and twiddle with the knobs and lenses to get the picture right. You have to move around, try all the angles. You must remember how much subject you can include, how much depth of field you have got, and keep an eye on what the light is doing.

35 mm cameras

I use a 35 mm outfit. There are three reasons: cost, weight and size. I want a minimum of three lenses, and alternative lenses are cheaper for 35 mm camera than any other. Also the film costs less per frame than larger sizes. In my own 'everyday' outfit I have three lenses, a flashgun, extension tubes, pistol-grip, flash bar, waist-level viewfinder, exposure meter and two rolls of film.

The weight is about 2 kg (12 lb) including the camera. An equivalent 6×6 cm ($2\frac{1}{4} \times 2\frac{1}{4}$ in) outfit would weight at least twice as much. That can matter a lot if you have to carry it around for a full day. An equivalent 110 outfit is much smaller and lighter, but the tiny negatives give little scope for selectively enlarging parts. In fact, anything larger than an album print is hard to make even from the full frame area.

Cameras

There is a bewildering range of 35 mm equipment on the market and selection can be a nightmare. If you are thinking about buying one, first of all handle it; hold it up to your eye, does it sit comfortably in your hand? Can you reach the shutter release button easily? When you fire the shutter, does the button move in smoothly and positively? Can you feel the slight extra pressure which actually fires the shutter? When it does fire, does the shutter move across smoothly and quietly, or does it shoot across with a bang that jerks the camera in your hand? If it feels all right when you use it, and you can afford it, what about accessories? Is there a good range of lenses, and are they of sufficiently good quality? Is the camera distributed by a well-established firm — it can be awkward if the firm goes out of business and you cannot get spares. If you do buy it, how many camera shops in the country stock it and how easy is it to get it repaired. If you plan to do a lot of travelling, find out in how many countries the equipment is sold. Last of all, look in the 'For sale' columns of the photographic press and see how much the equipment sells for. You can lose quite a lot of money if you choose to sell an unknown camera.

Single-lens reflex (SLR) or rangefinder?

Today, sophisticated 35 mm cameras are predominantly SLRs, which do have a considerable advantage over rangefinder models if you want to use extra-wide-angle or extra-long-focus lenses; or are interested in close-up photography, or using special accessories. Basically the SLR allows you to look through the taking lens of the camera, and see exactly what the film will see when the shutter is opened. If you change the lens or fit any special accessory, you still see exactly what the film will see, because you are looking through the taking lens (and its accessories). Also, there is no parallax problem when you are working close to your subject.

Range finder cameras have a separate viewfinder system with its own lenses. In general they are smaller than single-lens reflex cameras, because there is no need for a mirror between lens and film, which saves space, and the rangefinder is lower than the pentaprism through which you look in the SLR camera. You can get rangefinder cameras which will accept interchangeable lenses. On the most expensive, the viewfinder too changes automatically when you change lenses; on others, you have to carry an auxillary viewfinder for each lens.

There is also the problem of parallax, although the most expensive rangefinder cameras have built-in compensation for this. Although they are not as convenient as SLR cameras, they can be quite a bit smaller. I use an SLR normally, because it is more versatile; but my favourite camera is still a very elderly Leica Model 3. It is very small, very light, and it is a pleasure just to press the button.

Lenses

In my own opinion the most useful lenses to have are a 28 mm wide-angle lens, a 50 or 55 mm standard lens and a 105 mm telephoto.

Wide-angle a 28 mm lens is the best because it offers a much wider view from the standard lens. The once-popular choice of 35 mm focal length was largely governed by the shortcomings of lens design. Modern lenses offer much wider possibilities and the larger field of view can be very useful.

134

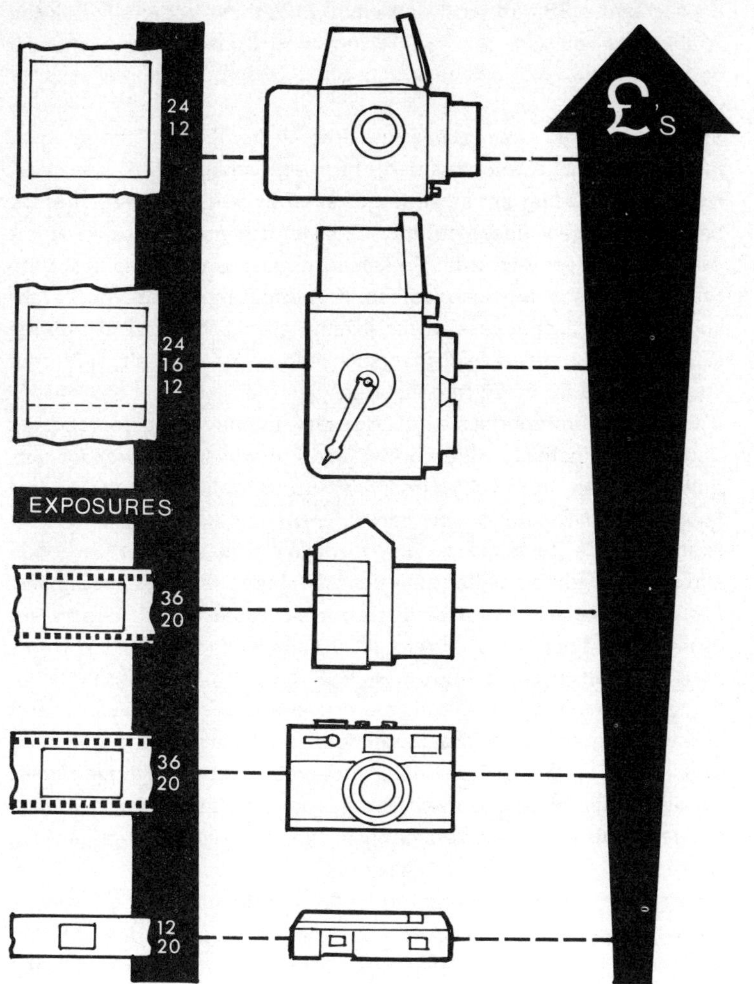

Five basic camera types. Cost relates directly to versatility. Roll film single lens reflex represents the ultimate sophistication in a hand camera. Twin lens reflex is much more restricted, but offers high quality results at reasonable cost. 35 mm single lens reflex gives all the picture quality most of us need, with extraordinary versatility. 35 mm compact has far fewer accessories, but offers the same picture quality. For simple everyday photography, the five symbol pocket camera is easy to use, and produces acceptable pocket-sized prints or small scale enlargements.

If you have a 28 mm lens, and want something wider still buy the widest one you can – a 17 or 18 mm lens if possible (or even a 13 or 15 mm one). Not a fisheye, though, unless you have real uses for it.

Standard lenses are usually the best value in any range. It is fashionable to overlook them, but with their wide apertures, reputation-building optics and natural viewpoint, consider carefully before you reject one. You may be able to choose between about 40 mm and nearly 60 mm. So select the one which goes best with the other lenses you want to use. If you feel that an 80 or 90 mm suits you well, choose a 40 or 45 mm standard, and a nice wide (20–24 mm) wide angle. Conversely, if you work a lot with a 28 mm lens, go for a 50 or 55 mm standard.

If the maximum aperture is unnecessary, look at a 'macro' focusing 50 mm lens instead of the normal one. It works just as well for normal work, and gives you added close-up capabilities.

Long-focus lenses produce narrow-angle pictures. Most modern examples are telephotos, which means that their construction allows them to be smaller than their focal length otherwise implies. For convenience, all longer-than-normal focal length lenses are often called 'telephotos'. I prefer a 105 mm lens to the 135 mm normally chosen, useful though that is. Simply, it has a slightly wider angle of view which makes it more useful when working in towns and villages. Very long focal length lenses are wonderful status symbols, but they do not have much use when photographing places. So, unless you want to use them for ornithology or sports work, I suggest you carry a 2x converter, or hire a 200 mm or longer lens for the few occasions you might need it.

Zoom lenses are becoming more and more popular, and deservedly so. One zoom offers you a whole range of focal lengths. You can choose exactly the viewpoint you really want, and then alter the focal length to fill a transparency exactly.

Zooms suffer from two disadvantages. They have relatively small maximum apertures, and they are comparatively heavy and bulky. Despite that, there are times when they can save space, and even weight. Until recently, their optical performance was somewhat suspect, but more recent designs, especially in the medium-telephoto range are capable of turning in an excellent performance.

136

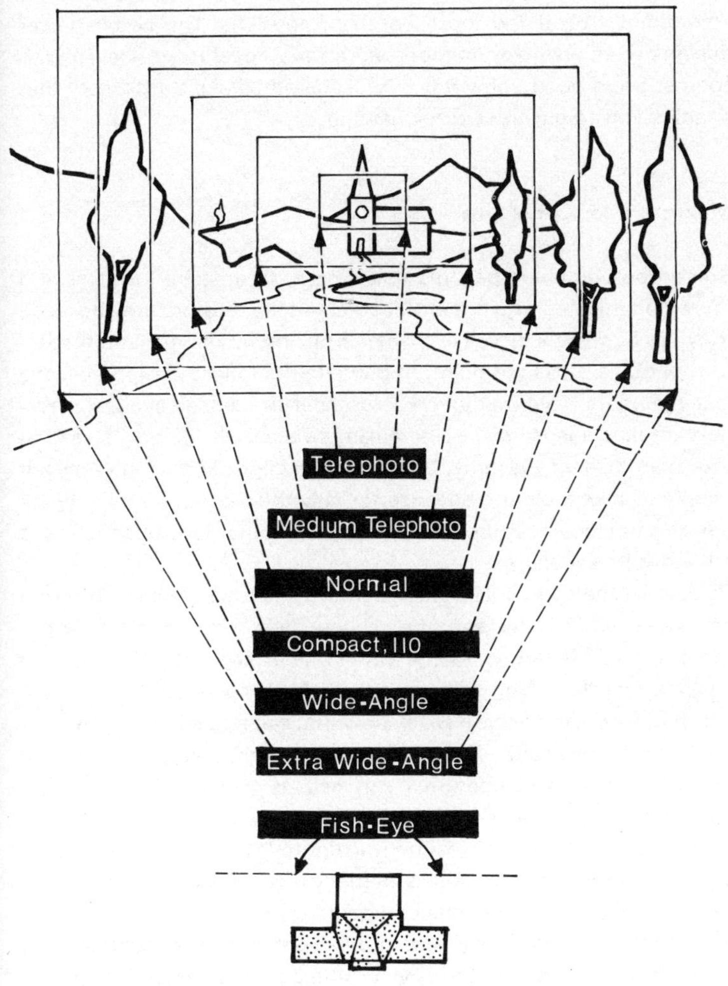

Interchangeable lenses alter the field of view. Wide-angle lenses let you get more in, and long focus lenses (telephoto) get a bigger picture—without moving.

Perhaps the most useful choice is around 80–200 mm, but if you consistently use the wider-angle end, 75–150 or even 50–135 are smaller, lighter alternatives.

Tele-converters are behind-the-lens accessories which double (or sometimes treble) the focal length of any lens. The better newer designs work well with longer-than-normal focal lengths even with zooms. So, a good converter is a useful small, light accessory that enables you to get the occasional shot.

Maximum lens aperture

Some photographers become obsessed with a desire for more and more complicated equipment. They also take less pictures because they are busy thinking up excuses for buying it. The maximum aperture battle is a case in point. Improvements in lens design over the last ten years have made very wide aperture lenses available. Yet, how often is a lens used at its maximum aperture? I had guessed at less than 10% of the time, but only a fortnight ago I found myself unable to take a picture because for only the second time in my life a maximum lens aperture of *f*2.8 was *just* not large enough to make a hand-held exposure.

Of course, there are occasions when there is too little light to take a picture, whatever the aperture of your lens. The important argument, though, is the occasions when one or two extra stops would allow a picture. If you think about it, they are very rare. Also the depth of field can become so shallow that the range of opportunities for using fantastically wide-aperture lenses is severely limited. The one time that wide apertures can help is when you use a tele-converter. These accessories reduce the effective *f*-number to double (2×) or treble (3×) its normal figure (*f*2.8 becomes *f*5.6 with a 2× converter for example). With many it is unwise to use full aperture, so a wide-aperture lens can help.

Despite that, it is normally best to choose the smallest aperture lens in the range and spend the saving on extra accessories. For example, it is possible to buy two *f*2.8 lenses, say one telephoto and one wide-angle, for the price of an *f*1.9 wide-angle lens. If you propose to use your camera mainly for pictures out of doors, and indoors with flash, then you will rarely find yourself using apertures of less than $f5.6$.

If you want to take pictures using available light, then use a time exposure and a tripod. The times when you can use neither are very limited.

Roll-film (120) cameras

Professional photographers use larger format cameras whenever they can. Principally because the finished negative or slide is considerably larger than that from a 35 mm camera. Since most professional work is either used in an enlarger to produce quite large prints (standard size is about 8 × 10 in), or used for photo-mechanical reproduction on the printed page, the extra size offers a lot of extra quality. And these cameras can still have the advantages of interchangeable lenses.

For amateur use, those advantages are less useful. With more time you can produce excellent prints of up to about 16 × 20 in from 35 mm negatives; and the fact that transparencies are larger means that you need a special projector. The choice is limited and most are very expensive. However, 120 size cameras are used by many amateurs, especially those who do their own printing, and for whom quality is the main parameter.

Size 120 film is about 65 mm ($2\frac{1}{2}$ in) wide. All 120 cameras take pictures around 56 mm ($2\frac{1}{4}$ in) wide, but the length varies from type to type. The most popular size is square – about 56 × 56 mm ($2\frac{1}{4}$ × $2\frac{1}{4}$ in) – called 6 × 6 cm. The original size was 56 × 85 mm ($2\frac{1}{4}$ × $3\frac{1}{4}$ in) – called 6 × 9 cm. A number of recent cameras use frames closer in shape to printing papers: 56 × 70 mm, called 6 × 7 cm, and 56 × 46 mm, called 6 × 4.5 cm.

Some people find that the square format allows them much more freedom in framing their pictures, particularly since they can make the final framing after the film has been processed, either by masking their transparencies or by selecting the picture on the enlarger easel. I find that, given a square viewfinder, I frame a square picture and have nothing spare for masking afterwards.

Really, modern 6 × 7 cm cameras are too bulky to carry around, though they are excellent in the studio. So the alternative to a square format is 6 x 4.5 cm. There are several excellent single-lens reflexes in this size. They offer a good compromise between size and quality if you like an oblong viewfinder. However, at waist-level, you are limited to horizontal pictures.

In 6 x 6 cm cameras, you can choose between single-lens reflexes, the best of which are unbeatable for photographing places, but rather more expensive than most people want; and twin-lens reflexes. Twin-lens reflexes are excellent 'starter' cameras for black-and-white work, but only one, the Mamiya C330 and its relatives, offers lens interchangeability. If you make prints, and want to use a fixed-lens camera think about using a wide-angle roll-film one. It can offer great scope.

The most useful alternative lenses for 6 x 6 cm ($2\frac{1}{4}$ x $2\frac{1}{4}$ in) are 50 mm for wide-angle and 150 mm or 160 mm long-focus. Longer and shorter lenses are available, but they again have a limited use for photographing places, and are probably better hired.

Because the choice of cameras is limited in this format, the choice of lenses is equally limited, and the cheap, high quality alternatives which are available in the 35 mm format do not exist. Lenses are, therefore, much more expensive. All the equipment is much bulkier, and is usually heavier.

Apart from the ease of producing prints (even laboratories offer a better and cheaper service to the professional) from roll-film negatives, such cameras are of particular value to those who would like to make their photography pay. These larger sizes of transparency are easier to sell than are 35 mm transparencies.

There is no way to produce a positive recommendation about which camera you should buy. Consider the cost, spend slightly less than you can afford, so that you have some left over for the accessories you are sure to need within the first few months of buying a camera. Decide on the type of photography you are most interested in. Look at the sort of equipment available. But then you have to go to a shop and look them over.

Meters also vary. My own camera has spot TTL metering—it measures the light falling on a particular spot in the viewfinder, and it does it through the lens. I also carry a separate meter with an attachment for incident light meter readings. I suppose I carry that meter because I have owned it for the whole of my time in photography and I know I can rely on the readings.

Also in my gadget bag are *two* lens brushes: one for cleaning the inside of the camera body, the other for cleaning the lens, and they are clearly marked to show which is which. I do that to stop the dust from the camera body scratching the lens.

Gadgets

Gadgets come and go in photography as much as any other hobby. This year's wonder gadget becomes next year's piece of unused gear. Most of them have a limited use, and once the possibilities for using a gadget in your photography has gone, then it can be discarded. I can think of some very expensive gadgets I have used over the last two years – a multiple image attachments was one. I had finished with it in two days, but those pictures were very interesting. Fortunately, I managed to borrow it, so it left me none the poorer. However, there are a few attachments which are relatively cheap, and seem to earn their living every now and then.

Fog filters are designed to simulate the effect of misty mornings. They give a misty effect, of course, but the probelm with them is that they give the same mist effect over the whole subject, where a real mist gets thicker the further away from the subject you get. They are probably most useful if you have a subject which has a high contrast foreground, with a background you do not want to see in detail. I have found them more useful in parks within towns than in the countryside.

To get the most out of them I would suggest making up a matte box and cutting the filter. By moving the filter further away from the lens the effect can be localized to the part of the picture you want. Buy the filter in gel form, not mounted between glass, and mount it so that it covers only part of the image. Rotate the matte box until the filter lines up with the straight line break in the subject – such as the side of a road, close to the camera and the effect is greatly improved. The nearest objects are clear, and objects further away become misty. Keep the filter as flat as possible in the matte box and do not use it when there is a lot of strong sunlight about because it will seriously degrade the image in those conditions because of light reflected from the back of the filter. When using a fog filter over the whole lens, make some allowance in your exposure. When using a partial filter in a matte box, do not make any allowance for the filter. Of course, in either case you can rely on through-the-lens measurement with no compensation.

Polarizing filters

Polarizing filters can be used directly on the camera lens, and can be bought mounted in glass, ready to fit. They have two uses, one for landscapes, and another when in towns. In the countryside they can be used to make skies darker. They increase the density of the blue sky, and make it get darker towards the top of the picture. They have most effect when photographing at right angles to the sun, that is when the sun is shining directly toward one of your shoulders. The only way of judging the effect is by looking through the filter. If you have a single-lens reflex camera, this is no problem, simply fit it over the camera lens and look through the viewfinder. If you have a twin-lens reflex, fit it over the *viewing* lens and rotate the filter until you get maximum effect. Then note the angle of the filter, and transfer it to the taking lens, making sure that the filter is at the same angle it was on the viewing lens. If you have a rangefinder type camera, look through the filter and rotate it until you get maximum darkening effect – then put it over the lens, again making sure that the filter is at the same angle when fitted over the lens as it was when you were looking through it. In all these cases, beware moving the angle of the filter after it has been fitted. If you do, the effect will be reduced, or eliminated.

On some cameras, you may find that the front of the lens mount rotates when you are focusing. This, of course, changes the angle of the filter. With this sort of camera, focus first and fit the filter afterwards. When using one of these filters you will need to make an allowance in your exposure for the density of the filter.

Contrast filters

When using black-and-white film it is possible to alter the contrast of the subject by using coloured filters over the camera lens.

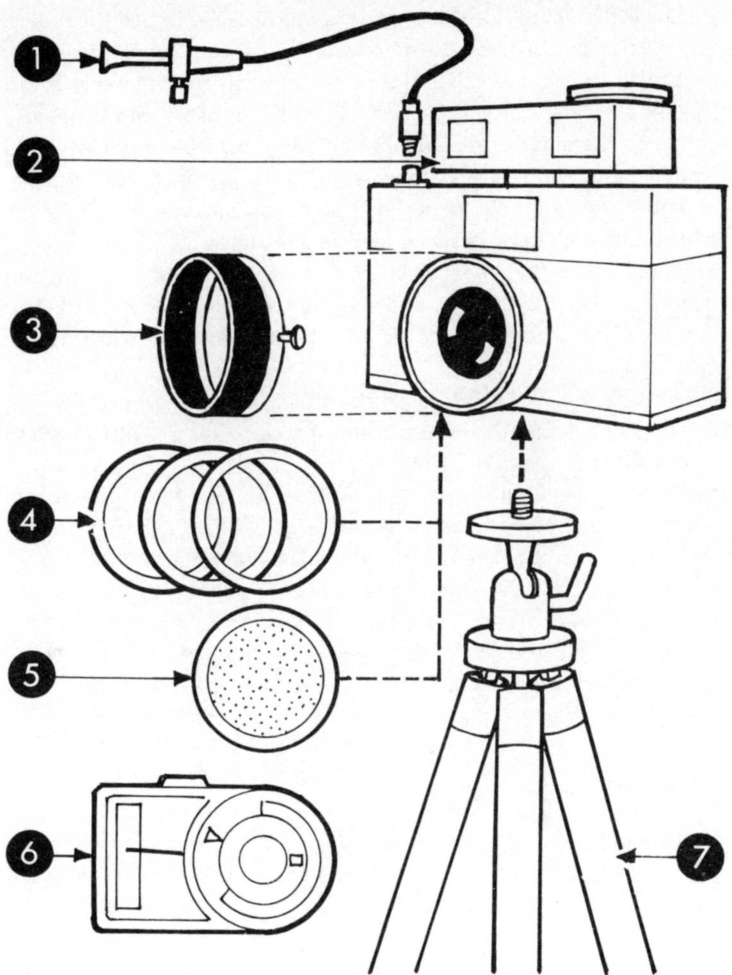

Even the simplest camera can be supplemented by some accessories. Of course, many are built into more sophisticated models, so you do not have to duplicate them. 1. A cable release is almost essential for long exposures. 2. A separate rangefinder is a great help with a simple direct-vision camera. 3. Always use a lens hood to avoid flare and protect the lens. 4. Close-up lenses offer lightweight close-up capability. 5. The choice of filters depends on film and subject. 6. A hand-held light meter helps in difficult situations even with automatic exposure. 7. A tripod is the most convenient camera support.

Because the filters are coloured, it is not possible to use them with any sort of colour film. The filter works in a very simple way. Any part of the subject which is the same colour as the filter comes out lighter, and any part of the subject which is of a complementary colour to the subject appears darker. The most used contrast filters for black-and-white are yellow and red. The sort of range normally carried is: yellow – $1\frac{1}{2}$, 4; red – 2, 4. If you become very involved with the technique, a green 4 can be useful.

Yellow filters make landscapes, particularly ones with lots of green vegetation, slightly lighter, and the blue sky above them darker. It has no effect on the clouds. The bigger the number following the filter, the bigger the effect.

Green filters have a more gentle effect on landscapes, and the finished picture looks more normal than one taken with a strong yellow filter.

Red filters have a more spectacular effect, but they are more useful when photographing deserts or buildings, which have more red in their natural colour. They render the sky almost black.

When using any of these filters, make an allowance in your exposure. The numbers I have referred to are the filter factors of the filters and *not* the manufacturer's code number. These will be different from manufacturer to manufacturer. All these filters will work at any angle to the sun.

Haze filters

These can be invaluable with any sort of film. There are two types, one absorbs UV light only, and has a gentle effect on the finished picture. The other has a slight pink colour, usually referred to as a 1A filter, it makes the picture slightly less blue. For low level work, the UV filter is perfectly adequate, although you may prefer the slightly warmer colours produced when the 1A filter is used. I would recommend keeping one or the other over all your lenses to keep dust from the optical surface of the lens. They are easier to clean and less expensive to replace if an accident happens. Neither filter needs any allowance in the exposure. Do take them off, though when you take pictures against the light, any filter will increase the chance of flare effects.

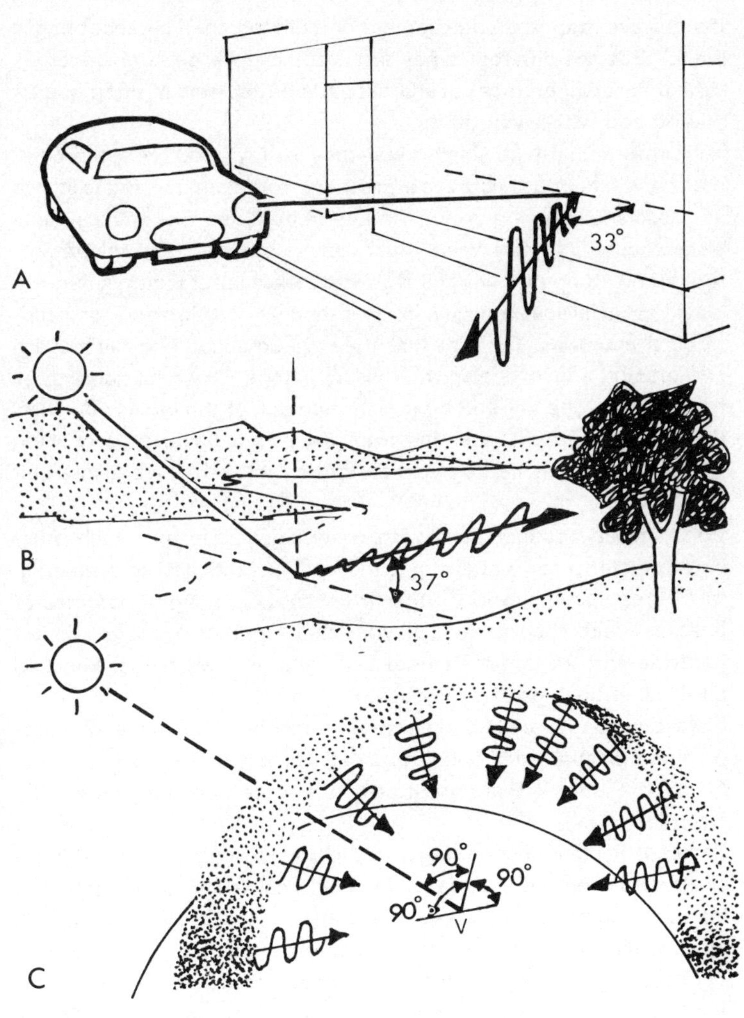

Natural sources of polarized light. A, Light reflected at about 33° from glass is polarized. B, So is light reflected at about 37° from water. C, A band of skylight is strongly polarized.

Gadget bags

If you have more than one camera and/or lens, then a gadget bag is useful. But the different types and sizes can be quite bewildering. Which sort will be most useful depends on the sort of photography you do and where you do it.

The professional-type shiny metal case is very good for both equipment and film. It protects the equipment from damage, and is strong and resilient, standing up well to lots of hard use. The shiny surface also reflects light and *heat*, which seems to be increasingly important when storing modern films. If you take a lot of pictures they are ideal, especially if you live in or intend to visit tropical or semi-tropical countries. The fact that they are so solid, with fairly sharp corners and edges, is also their disadvantage. They can do damage to the inside of a car and hit you in the back of the leg as you carry them. If you are not working from a car, but have to carry them round all day they can be very uncomfortable. They are also a bait for thieves.

Soft, squashy gadget bags with a shoulder strap are much more comfortable to carry about, but they offer practically no protection for the equipment inside, either from knocks, or from extremes of heat and cold. They do keep all your gear together, and if you do not take the sort of pictures where your gear is likely to get knocked about, then they can be very useful.

I discovered an almost ideal case recently; it is made of light-coloured plastic, with round, moulded corners and curved to fit the hip. But it is not a waterproof case; there are two holes where the strap fits.

The case is foam lined, to keep all the pieces of equipment separate and safe. Doing this wastes space; but because my camera travels a lot, and some knocks are inevitable, I think the sacrifice is worthwhile. I always travel with my camera with a lens fitted around my neck not in the case. This means that I can take a picture quickly if I see one, or change lenses and select accessories if I need to and have the time. I also have separate cases for each lens so that I can go out with the camera round my neck and a second lens safely in my pocket, but many people would consider that of marginal value.

Tripods

A tripod is a useful addition to any set of photographic equipment. It allows an increased range of pictures to be taken, particularly at low light levels. Typical subjects would be night shots, or the interiors of buildings.

Camera shake is also eliminated if you use a tripod. This is more of a problem than most people recognize. Not the very bad shake which is instantly recognizable, but the very slight shake which slightly affects the sharpness of the picture. This can be present in pictures taken at shutter speeds up to 1/125 second. A good tripod eliminates this problem.

What is a good tripod? A heavy one! There is no substitute for weight in a tripod, because steadiness is related to the overall weight of the camera and tripod. That also means, unfortunately, that the lighter the camera, the more you need a heavy tripod. There are ways of adding to the overall weight of a tripod without having more weight to carry. For example, if it is not too windy, a gadget bag can be hung from the tripod, which will help to steady the whole assembly.

Light tripods are, however, much better than nothing, except in a strong wind, when the camera would probably be steadier if you held it. Make sure that the tripod has strong legs, with secure locking devices on them. When the legs are fully extended, press downwards on the top of the tripod. The legs should not bend or splay outwards. Rubber feet are almost always better than metal ones. The best type have a retractable metal spike inside the rubber feet.

Tripod heads for still photography a ball-and-socket head is prefectly adequate, but it is a little awkward to use. A pan-and-tilt head is probably less satisfactory, because when using it, the tripod legs have to be adjusted to make the camera level. A pan-tilt-and-rocker head is undoubtedly the most satisfactory. It is also suitable for ciné work. Anything else attached to a tripod is a luxury.

So, the points to look for in a tripod are:

1   Sturdy non-slip feet.

2   Easily adjustable legs with secure locking devices.

3   Sturdy legs which do not splay or bend when you press down on them.

4   Fitted with, or designed to take, either a ball-and-socket head or a pan-tilt-and-rocker head.

5   If in doubt, choose the heavier tripod.

Choosing a Film

Everyone has different ideas about how their pictures should look. Some films will give a cool bluish look, if you want your pictures to look like that – fine! Others make a pink skin-tone look brown and tanned; fine if you only photograph girls in bikinis, but green grass looks brown, and the sky looks as though there is a forest fire not far away.

Obviously the first question about choosing a film is 'which is the best?'. The answer is not simple. Many photographic magazines publish comparisons of various types and makes of film, and they can form a useful guide. It is possible to measure things like resolving power – the ability of the film to record fine detail, but they cannot put a number to the way the finished pictures look. The way the eye sees colour is subtly different to the way a film sees it, and manufacturers design their films to record the common colours most faithfully, and the less common colours can be a little 'wrong'. So you have to choose for yourself the film which gives colours which *you* think are the most realistic. Try two or three manufacturer's products. Take pictures of similar sorts of subject: a landscape, a flower-bed, a close-up of a person; and compare the results. Decide which film you like best and stick to it.

You can only improve your photography by taking pictures, looking critically at the results and learning from them. If you continually change the make of film you use, then direct comparisons can be meaningless. So make your decision about manufacturer and then stick to it. Of course, if new films appear, there is no harm in trying them, but try to maintain a consistent choice of film for the majority of your work.

Each manufacturer makes a whole range of films and you have to decide which of their films you should use for a particular assignment. Colour or black-and-white? That should be easy, so let's look at choosing a colour film first.

Choosing a colour film

Prints or slides? It is a difficult choice which depends a lot on personal preference and what you want to do with the finished pictures. A print is a lot easier to look at; slip it out of its wallet and there it is. Slides need a viewer, or, to get the best out of them, a projector and a darkened room.

Quality also comes into it. The depth of colour, detail in shadows and areas of bright light are much better on slides than on prints. Graininess, the small blobs which appear in a colour picture, is usually more noticeable in negatives than it is in slide material of the same speed.

Correct *exposure* is not as critical on negative material as it is on slides, for example, Kodak recommend that exposure for their colour negative materials is from $\frac{1}{2}$ stop under to 2 stops over exposure; although accurate exposure obviously produced the best results. Colour slides however must not be more than $\frac{1}{2}$ stop under or over exposure and for the best results less than that. Mistakes in exposure can be corrected on colour negative materials when they are printed. There is virtually nothing you can do to correct badly exposed transparencies. The fact that you can 'correct' for colour and exposure does mean however that some prints will look awful if you have them made commercially. This is not your fault, it is just that the printer has 'corrected' wrongly.

In general if you have confidence in your ability to expose every picture correctly and quality comes first, use a slide film. You can get prints if you want them — they will cost you slightly more than prints from negatives, but you can see exactly what the picture looks like as a slide and only get prints from the best pictures of the set.

You may find the quality of prints from slides slightly disappointing. In the main this is because the quality of the slide picture is so much better than it is possible to get from any print.

If you cannot guarantee absolutely accurate exposure every time, if you do not ever plan to give a slide show, and if you want a record of what you did and where you went, then try a negative material. But you have to have each negative printed because you cannot tell much from looking at a colour negative. Remember that you can get colour slides from colour negatives, and you can get excellent black-

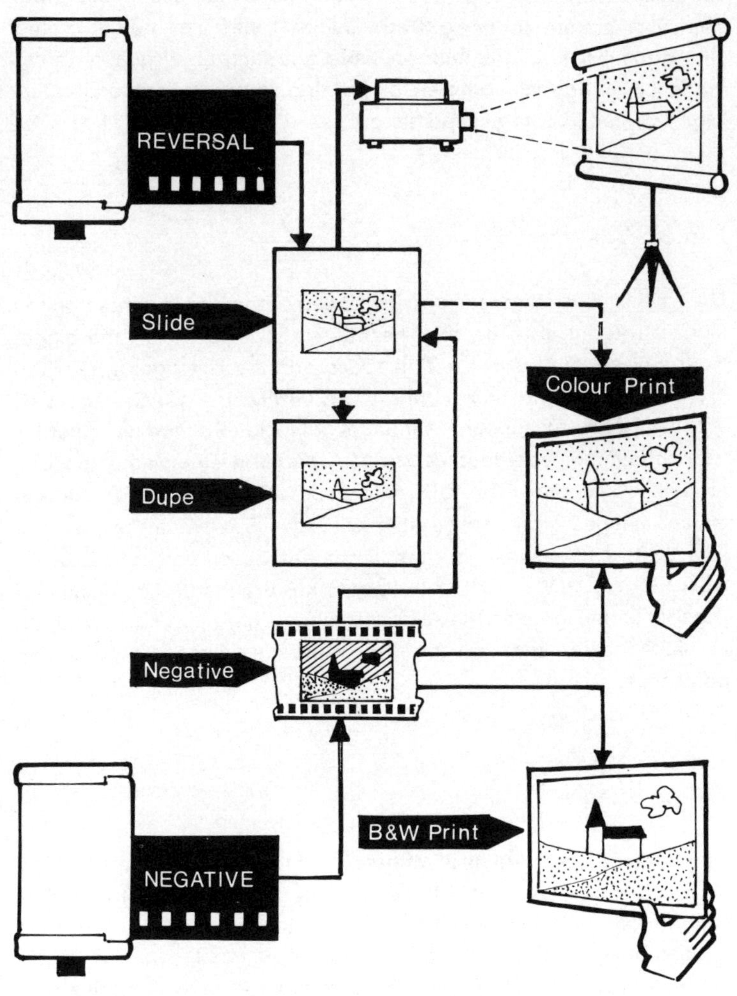

Colour films are commonly available to give either as reversal (slide) or negative emulsions. Choose the one that produces what you want. You can, though, make prints from slides or slides from negatives.

and-white prints too. The range of film speeds available is much more limited, but most colour negative films can be considerably underexposed without too bad a result. I have had reasonable prints from film 3 stops underexposed – but that was very new film and very good printing. I would not have got such good quality prints made by a normal commercial printing, but $1\frac{1}{2}$–2 stops under-exposed should give acceptable prints.

Film speeds

Now what about film speeds? The speed of the film is printed on the side of the film box, usually like this – ASA.../DIN... – the bigger the numbers the faster the film speed and the less light it needs to make pictures. The two numbers are different, e.g. ASA 125/DIN 22. The ASA (American Standards Association) number doubles when the film speed doubles. An ASA 250 film is twice the speed of an ASA 125 film. The DIN (Deutsche Industrie Norm) number trebles when the film speed doubles: DIN 25 is twice the speed of DIN 22 (the series is logarithmic). The film speed may be shown as ASA/ISO ... DIN .... ISO (International Standards Organisation); the ISO is the same as the ASA. If you have a meter or camera with an ASA scale, just set the ISO numbers instead, there is no difference.

Colour balance

The sort of *light* which illuminates your subject is important for slides. Normally you should use daylight type film for outdoor work (and indoor work using flash). If you are taking indoor pictures with tungsten lighting (normal light bulbs, not flash) you should use tungsten or type B films. You can continue to use daylight film with tungsten light if you place a type 80A Filter over the camera lens; allow for the filter when you set the exposure meter. With a colour negative film there is no problem because better compensation is made when the negatives are printed.

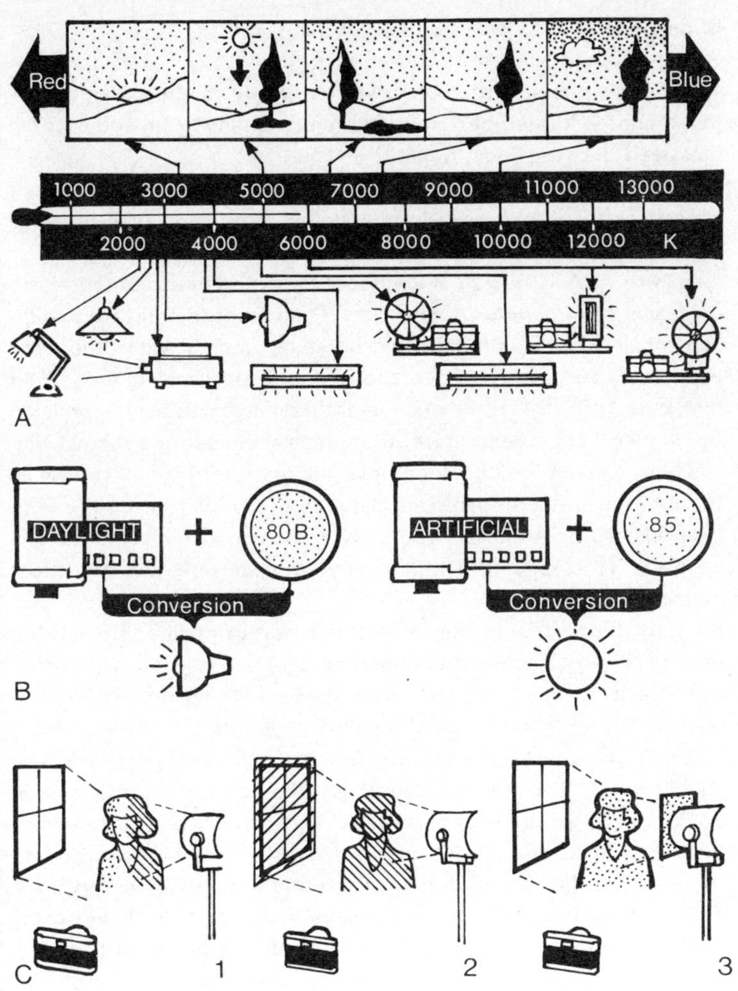

What we see as 'white' light can vary quite considerably in colour. A. The colour of lighting is often expressed as its colour temperature in kelvins (K). Daylight film is balanced for about 5500K, and tungsten light film for 3200 K.B. If you use the 'wrong' film, you can balance the colour with a filter, often given a 'wratten' number. C. If you mix lighting, your pictures will look bicoloured. (1) You can filter the daylight orange (2) or the tungsten light blue (3), and use the appropriate film to get natural-looking pictures.

Slide films

Think about the sort of subject you are likely to photograph. How much light will there be? How much movement in the subject? Do you need the very finest quality?

Reversal films fall into three broad groups according to their speed – fast, medium and slow. A slower film (lower ASA number) has finer grain and records more fine detail.

Fast films ASA 125–500. If you want to take pictures outdoors on a dull rainy day you want a fast film. If your subjects are likely to be fast moving, such as a galloping horse or running water, then you will need a fast shutter speed and in poor light that demands a fast film, over 125 ASA. How much over that magic number depends on the subject, but I would not automatically choose the fastest film available. Quality, colour, sharpness and graininess fall off rapidly as the film speed increases. You also have to be very accurate with your exposure. Although you may get away with slight under-exposure ($\frac{1}{2}$ stop at the most), any overexposure will ruin most pictures.

So you have to choose the slowest film that can still do the job but returns the best quality. If the light falls away rapidly it is sometimes possible to compensate for underexposure during processing, but you cannot do this with all slide films. If you have underexposed a fast film, tell your dealer by how much, e.g. if your meter said you should use *f*2 and the maximum aperture on your camera is *f*2.8, tell him that the film is underexposed by 1 stop. If you process your own films, the dealer or manufacturer will tell you if it is possible to increase the film speed during processing and, if so, how to do it. Fast films are very useful, but always think carefully before using them. For example, if you are going to photograph a dark interior scene, such as a church, the obvious choice is to go for a fast film. But if you are not trying to capture any movement – and you want the greatest detail possible – there is no reason why you should not choose the slowest film and use a tripod and a long time exposure. Do that and you can also use a very small aperture and get the maximum depth of field. Use a fast film when you want to photograph something which is moving in poor light conditions or if you have to hand-hold the camera.

Medium speed films ASA 50–100. A medium speed film is the obvious choice if you do not shoot a complete roll of film in one day or on one type of subject; if your subject matter is unpredictable; or if the weather is unpredictable. These films have excellent quality and colour reproduction, they record detail well and are slightly more tolerant of poor exposure, but $\frac{1}{2}$ stop under or over exposure is about the maximum for most subjects. They have enough speed to allow a fairly high shutter speed (few photographers can be sure of pin sharp pictures through a standard lens with exposures longer than 1/60 second) and still let you use a fairly small aperture which makes focusing less critical and gives more depth of field.

My ideal film speed is about 100 ASA. I can use fairly long telephoto lens and, in bright sunlight, shoot pictures of 1/500 second at *f*8. That shutter speed is fast enough for shaky hands and still gives a reasonable working aperture.

Slow speed films ASA 25–50. The very best quality and the finest image is obtained on slow speed colour films. They are less critical in exposure, and give much more detail, particularly in shadow areas. The latest films are very, very good. So why not use them all the time? Simply because they are slow. In bright light they are superb, but as soon as the light starts to fall, then you will be forced to use a slow shutter speed with the consequential risk of camera shake.

Slow films are ideal for use in snowy weather with the sun shining or on the beach, or at sea. They are equally useful if you intend to give long exposures with the camera firmly fixed on a tripod. I also use them when I want to get a large colour print from a small format camera, e.g. a 16 × 20 in print from a 35 mm slide, or a 30 × 40 in print from a 6 × 6 cm ($2\frac{1}{4}$ × $2\frac{1}{4}$ in) slide. They give better detail than a negative of an equivalent size.

To sum up then, use a *slow film* with a tripod-mounted camera, or with a hand-held camera in brilliant sunlight, when you want the very highest quality.

Work with a medium speed film most of the time, particularly if you cannot predict the sort of subject you are likely to take. And use high-speed film when working in poor light, particularly when using a high shutter speed. That is, whenever you have moving subjects, or want to use a telephoto lens.

Choosing a black-and-white film

We dealt with colour films first because most people use them. There is little cost advantage these days in using black-and-white, and for the same money you have all the wonder of colour, which is fine if you *want* colour, but you may not! Suppose that colour photography had been invented first, and that someone had devised a way to remove the colour, rendering the whole scene in terms of black, white and grey – it would be hailed as a new art form.

One of the main joys of taking black-and-white pictures is the control you have, particularly at the printing stage. If you get the chance, have a look at some prints made by a photographer at the turn of the century – Frank Sutcliffe of Whitby. The beauty of these pictures is amazing, so is the quality. He was fascinated by the sailing ships of the period, by clouds and sky, and by the life of the people. The play of light and shade, the depth of shadows and the detail, the shimmering light of a clear summer's day are so well captured. Colour simply cannot give the same sort of effect.

Another good reason for many people taking black-and-white is that many magazines and newspapers are prepared to pay for monochrome pictures, but do not want to buy colour.

Choosing a black-and-white film is very similar to choosing a colour film. They can be split into three groups – fast, medium and slow. The slower the film, the better the quality. Similarly, when in doubt, choose a medium speed film.

However, the real skill in choosing a black-and-white film is to match the developer, the film, the enlarger and the paper that you use. Everyone has a slightly different technique, and you will have to experiment until you find two or three films (slow, medium and fast, or just medium and fast) together with one or two developers (fine grain, or high-acutance and fine-grain).

Most of the problems associated with black-and-white photography are the result of constantly changing films and chemicals. Choose a film and developer and stick to it, then you can get used to working with it and go back to concentrating on your picture-making technique. The mechanical problems, if you want to call them that, should be sorted out and forgotten, leaving you free to express yourself photographically as fully as possible.

Looking after your films

Always buy your film from a shop which keeps the stock nice and cool, and out of direct sunlight; and keep your films in similar conditions. Bad storage can produce slightly odd colours, and the film might not be at quite the speed marked on the packet. Heat is particularly bad for any film. Once the packet has been opened the film can also be affected by humidity – steamy or damp conditions are not good for films. The basic storage rules are printed quite clearly on the packet.

Keep in a cool, dry place

Some films are easier to keep than others, in fact the manufacturer designs them that way. Every manufacturer makes some films he designates 'professional', sometimes they even incorporate the word into the title of the film. It does not mean that these films will give you better pictures, or even different ones. There is no magic to professional photography; it is a combination of good equipment, good technique and experience. If you want to try a professional film by all means do so. They are slightly more consistent than amateur products. The consistency is quite important for someone shooting thirty or forty rolls of film in a single day on the same sort of subject. For most people that sort of accuracy is not needed. If you do use them, they should be kept in a refrigerator before use, taken out of the refrigerator a few hours before it is to be used, and allowed to warm up. Then load, expose, unload and process as soon as possible.

Manufacturers presume that the other films (they never call them 'amateur' to their customers) will not be stored in a refrigerator, and will remain in the camera for some time. The film is made so that the changes which occur in the film actually improve it. This does not mean that the film will be even better if you bake it! You would ruin it, because the changes reach a peak and then deterioration sets in, but they are better for general use.

The rules for storing film are simple:

1   Keep it dry.

2   Keep it cool.

3   Get it processed as soon as you can.

This is not always simple, especially if you are away from home – on holiday for example. Hotels are not usually keen to keep your films in their refrigerators. Most rooms have a cool spot though, a wardrobe, for example, is usually fairly cool. Keep your supply of film there and just take enough with you each day. When you are out and about try to keep your films in the shade, and send them off for processing when you have finished. That way some of your holiday pictures may be waiting for you when you get home.

There are lots of don'ts:

1   Never leave your films in the glove compartment or the back window of a car. Even in a temperate country like England you can get temperatures of over 150 °F on the back window ledge of a car. Far too hot for films, even for a few hours.

2   Never leave a film in direct sunlight, even if it is shining through a window.

3   Never store films in a warm cupboard, near a radiator or an infra-red heater.

4   Never store films in damp places, such as bathrooms, especially if you have opened the packet. (Cameras do not care for that sort of treatment either.)

Taking your film through airports

The security devices installed at many airports include X-ray equipment. X-rays can affect photographic film in two ways. Not only can they fog unexposed film, they can, in certain circumstances wipe the image off exposed films. The first is the more common effect, and appears on the processed film as bars across the frame.

You can buy bags which claim to protect film from X-rays when passing through airports, but experience suggests that they offer little protection.

The *only* safe way of taking film through airports is to take it as hand luggage and have it visually inspected if required.

Index

Accessories 143
Activity 95
Aerial perspective 53
After dark 86
Against the light 111
Airports 159
Apertures 32, 138
Aperture priority metering 44
Architectural photography 71
Automatic exposure control 42

Beaches 102
Black-and-white films 156
Borders 30
Brickwork 73
Bright areas 46
Buildings 71/90
Built-in meters 40

Checking equipment 10
Choosing films 149
Churches 86
Climbing 118
Clouds 73
Coasts 102
Cold weather 152
Colour balance 152
Colour film 150
Colour temperature 121, 153
Complex cameras 11
Composition 15
Contrast filters 142
Converging verticals 76

Dark subjects 46
Details 99
Developers 156

Entertainments 130
Equipment 9, 132/135
Exposure 31/48, 68, 104

Films 120, 149/159
Film speed 152
Filters 142
Fisheye lenses 61
Flash 129, 130
Floodlights 124
Foregrounds 78
Formats 29
Frames 82

Gadgets 141
Gadget bags 146

Harbours 107
Haze filters 116
Houses 89

Ice 112
Incident-light metering 88
Indoor pictures 88, 127
Industry 96

Landmarks 94
Landscapes 49
Learning 13
Lenses 22. 80
Light 64
Light-coloured subjects 47
Lightning 125
Lights 123
Long exposures 122
Long-focus lens 136

Measuring exposure 34
Moonlight 126
Mountains 116

Night pictures 120

Over ride controls 45

Painting with light   131
Panoramas   61
Planning pictures   13
People   85. 90, 100, 107
Perspective   23, 50
Polarizing filter   142
Printing in   63/64
Purpose   26

Rangefinder cameras   134
Rising front   77
Rivers   59
Roll-film cameras   139
Rules   18

Sea   108
Seasons   64
Selecting the picture   75
Separate meters   36
Shape   93
Shift lens   77
Shutter speeds   31, 57
Simple cameras   10, 132
Single-lens reflex   134
Skylight   114
Slide films   153

Snapshots   24, 103
Snow   112
Sports   128
Standard lens   136
Story pictures   27
Streets   94
Street lighting   122
Subjects   26
Sun   64, 114
Sunrises   66
Sunsets   66
Surfaces   72
Surroundings   74

Telephoto lens   24
35 mm cameras   133
Through-the-lens meters   41
Townscapes   91/101
Traffic   97
Tripods   147

Viewpoint   17

Water   56
Wide-angle lens   23